Veggie Haven

By Kentaro Kobayashi

Photography by Hideo Sawai

VERTICAL.

Contents

Numbers in parentheses indicate recipe page

Romaine Lettuce

Cilantro

Endive

56 Bountiful Main Dishes

88 Heartwarming Soups

100 Pasta! Pasta!

Reference Guide

Mizuna

Basil

Turnip Greens

Arugula

Watercress

Gentle and Delicious, the Power of Veggies

One day, I surprised myself with the flavor of a vegetable curry I had made. I always eat big, hearty meat dishes, but for some reason that day I wasn't in the mood for meat. I was amazed at how good the vegetables were. They gave the curry a subtle, yet truly delicious flavor.

That's how I decided to write this book.

That delicious, filling, vegetable curry.

My family always ate a lot of vegetable side dishes and I've always liked to eat my greens, but I really like meat, too. When people ask me, "Which do you like better, meat or vegetables?" I'm always at a loss for words because I don't compare them that way. But on that day, that curry showed me the true power of vegetables. And so I wanted to write a book dedicated to vegetable-centric dishes.

That's why there's no meat in these recipes.

Of course, it's not like I'm a vegetarian. I have lots of meals with meat *and* vegetables that are simply delicious, and nothing beats a good steak sometimes. But that's not what this book is about. I also use dried seafood, canned fish and milk products in some of the recipes.

So, here comes a whole bunch of veggies. But it's not just about eating healthy. I'd like to take some time to pay my respect to vegetables, to reveal the power behind them. This book is about vegetables written by a grateful fan.

Summer Vegetable and Bean Curry

Veggies are all you need for a rich flavor!

Cut large, hearty slices of vegetables and stew thoroughly. That's all it takes. All you have to do is stew! You'll be surprised at how good something so simple tastes. The only thing you need is time. The sweetness of the beans is satisfying, and fresh vegetables make a phenomenal curry.

The base is onions fried 'til brown

Ingredients (Serves 4)

16 oz (450 g) beans (fresh, dried or canned)
1 zucchini
1 carrot, peeled
2 stalks celery
1 each red, green and yellow bell peppers
1 onion
2 cloves of garlic
2 Tbsp olive oil
8 1/2 C water

A
- 3 leaves each fresh thyme, rosemary
- 1 tsp each oregano, basil (dried)

Curry Paste

3 onions
4 to 5 chili peppers

B
- 1 1/2 Tbsp curry powder
- 1/2 tsp each garam masala, coriander powder, cumin powder
- Dash red pepper

3 Tbsp oil
1/2 C tomato puree
1 tsp each soy sauce, salt, sugar

Salt and sugar, to taste
Steamed rice or naan bread

Instructions

1. Cut vegetables into chunks (photo 1). Cut garlic in half and crush with flat of knife.
2. Pour oil into a heated pan and sauté garlic over medium heat until fragrant. Add vegetables and sauté on high. Once vegetables are coated with oil, add water and mixture A, and stir-fry (photo 2). If you can't add all the water at once, add as much as possible then add gradually while cooking. Bring to a boil, then lower the heat and skim off any foam. Stew for 2 to 3 hours.

Delectable Vegetable Curries

If you think a vegetable-only curry is boring, think again.
The flavors are delicate, certainly, but the veggies lend their unique savor and richness.
The main thing to focus on is allowing plenty of time to let the curry sit and stew away.

3. Make curry paste: thinly slice onion. Remove stems from chili peppers and tear into pieces, seeds included. Add oil to a heated pan, add onions and sauté on high. When the onions are lightly browned, turn the heat to low and stir thoroughly (photo 3). Add mixture B, chili peppers, tomato puree, soy sauce, salt and sugar. Sauté over medium heat until it's paste-like in texture. Add 2 to 3 ladlefuls of the soup and stir until dissolved (photo 4).

4. Pour ingredients from step 2 into a bowl. Return 5 C of the soup base only to the pot. (If there's not enough liquid, add water). Return the vegetables to the pot and add curry paste from step 3. Rinse beans and dry, then add to mixture (photo 5). Stew for 1 hour on low heat, stirring occasionally. Season with salt and sugar to taste.

5. On a plate, add rice and pile the curry on top or serve naan bread on the side.

Note
Use any kind of bean. I've used white kidney beans, pinto beans, lentils and chickpeas in this recipe.

Winter Vegetables and Soybean Curry

The deep flavor of winter vegetables

It doesn't seem like daikon and burdock root would be good in curry, but they're actually quite tasty. A delicious richness slowly grown from the earth. Cutting them up then stewing thoroughly for a few hours will bring out their savory goodness. The secret to it is using the full-bodied red miso.

Good even when chilled!

Ingredients (Serves 4)

15oz (450 g) soybeans
    (canned or steamed)
3" daikon
1 carrot
1 burdock root
1 onion
4 to 5 cloves garlic
2 Tbsp oil
8 1/2 C water
1 bay leaf

Curry Paste

3 onions
2 to 3 Tbsp curry powder
A ⎡ 1 Tbsp each red miso, soy
    ⎢   sauce, sake, garam masala
    ⎣ 1 tsp salt, sugar
3 Tbsp oil
Salt and sugar, to taste
Rice or naan bread and sliced leeks,
    to taste

Instructions

1. Peel carrots and daikon, and clean burdock root with a scrub brush. Cut everything into bite-size pieces and thinly slice onions (photo 1).
2. Pour oil into a heated pan and sauté garlic over low heat until fragrant. Add vegetables and stir-fry over high heat until evenly coated with oil (photo 2). Add water (if you can't add it all at once, then add gradually while stir-frying) and bay leaf. Bring to a boil, lower heat and skim off any foam. Stew thoroughly for 2 to 3 hours.
3. Make the curry paste. Thinly slice the onion. Add oil to a heated pan. Add onions and sauté on high heat until tender. Turn heat to low and stir thoroughly (photo 3). Once onions are lightly browned, add mixture A. Sauté over medium heat until paste-like. Add 2 to 3 ladlefuls of the soup from 2 and stir until dissolved (photo 4).
4. Pour ingredients from step 2 into a bowl. Return 5 C of the soup base only to the pot. (If there's not enough liquid, add water). Return the vegetables to the pot and add curry paste from step 3 (photo 5). Rinse beans and dry, then add to curry. Stew for 1 hour over low heat, stirring occasionally. Season with salt and sugar to taste.
5. On a plate, add rice and pile the curry on top, and garnish with leek slices.

Eggplant and Coconut Milk Curry

Sweet and creamy eggplant curry!

Coconut milk is a surprisingly good complement for eggplant. Chives and deep-fried tofu are a great match for Asian-style seasonings. You can always use cream or milk, too. It's a quick and easy, one-pan kind of meal.

Chives go in last!

Ingredients (Serves 4)

4 to 5 eggplants (the small, slender Japanese or Italian type)
1 bunch garlic chives
1 block deep-fried tofu (*atsuage*. Or sub. Tofu Cutlet)
4 boiled eggs, shelled
3 cloves garlic
2 Tbsp oil
1 Tbsp Doubanjiang (Chinese chili paste)
2 Tbsp sake
1 Tbsp curry powder (heaping)
1 can (14 oz (400 g)) coconut milk
A ⎡ 3 kieffer lime leaves (or lemon zest)
  | 1 slice galangal root (or ginger, thinly sliced)
  ⎣ 4 to 5 stalks dried lemongrass
1/2 Tbsp sugar
Salt, nam pla (Thai fish sauce) and coriander, to taste
4 bowls freshly steamed rice

Instructions

1. Peel eggplants, quarter lengthwise and soak in salt water for 5 minutes. Cut chives into 2" (5 cm) slices, cut deep-fried tofu into 1/5" (5 mm) slices, and finely chop garlic (photo 1).
2. Pour oil into heated pan and sauté garlic until fragrant. Add Doubanjiang and stir (photo 2). Sauté on low until fragrant. Pat eggplants dry and stir-fry on high until tender. Add deep-fried tofu and stir-fry.
3. Add sake and stir briefly. Add curry powder (photo 3). When the powder has evenly coated everything, add coconut milk (photo 4), mixture A and boiled eggs. Simmer on medium heat until eggplants are tender (photo 5).
4. Add sugar and stir. Season with nam pla and salt. Add chives and simmer briefly. Serve over a bed of rice. Finish with coriander.

Note

Kieffer lime leaves and galangal root are common ingredients in Thai cuisine and can be found in Asian markets.

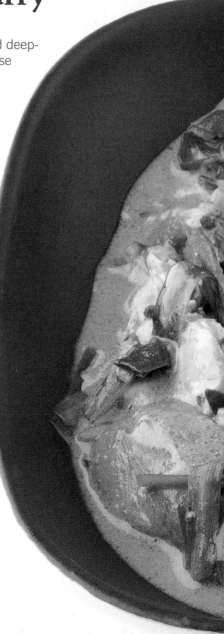

Satisfying Salads

When it comes to vegetables, we all think of salad. But plain old salad doesn't have any *oomph* to it. So, here's some satisfying twists to add heartiness to your salads.

Caesar Salad
Crunch away!

As soon as I find fresh romaine lettuce, I buy it to make Caesar salad. Big, chunky leaves of lettuce are always delicious. Whether you dive in straight away or eat it delicately with a knife and fork, it's scrumptious. Soak the croutons in garlic oil and grill to a perfect crunch. Coat the lettuce in dressing, sprinkle with croutons, add some shavings of Parmesan and finish with ground pepper. If you can't get your hands on a block of parmesan, you can always use the powdered version.

Ingredients (Serves 2 to 4)

1 head romaine lettuce
3 1/2" (8 cm) baguette bread
Block Parmesan cheese
Dash each salt and pepper

Garlic oil for croutons

Dash grated garlic
3 Tbsp olive oil
Pinch salt
Dash pepper

Dressing

3 heaping Tbsp grated
   Parmesan cheese
Dash grated garlic
1 1/2 Tbsp olive oil
1 1/2 Tbsp vinegar
1 Tbsp mayonnaise
1/2 Tbsp milk
2 pinches salt
Pinch sugar
Salt and pepper, to taste

Insalata Caprese

Use juicy tomatoes!

When it comes to tomatoes and basil, this is the definitive dish: Insalata Caprese. Here, I use plum tomatoes that have an intense sweetness. Slice up the mozzarella and tomatoes, and pull off the basil leaves. Arrange the tomatoes, mozzarella and basil on a dish, dress with oil and vinegar, and sprinkle with salt and pepper. The dressing is simple, too. Try adding it to your repertoire.

Ingredients (Serves 2)

5 leaves fresh basil
1 plum tomato (or regular tomato)
1/2 round (appx. 2 oz (50 g))
   fresh mozzarella cheese

Dressing

Dash grated garlic
1 Tbsp each olive oil and vinegar
2 pinches salt
Pepper, to taste

Warm Broccoli
and Potato Salad
Cubed vegetables tossed in a warm dressing!

Broccoli is great raw, so just blanch for 15 seconds or so. A little crunchiness is delicious.
Boil the potatoes until a skewer can be easily inserted. Drain. Make dressing in a pan.
Sauté garlic until golden, then add white wine. Turn off heat, add butter, sugar, salt and pepper.
Mix well, then add cheese. Add dressing to vegetables and toss.

Ingredients (Serves 4)
2 potatoes
1 head broccoli

Dressing
1 clove garlic
1/2 Tbsp oil
1/2 Tbsp white wine
1 1/2 Tbsp butter
2 pinches sugar
Salt and pepper, to taste

Potato Salad with Tuna and Olives

The essential potato dish

The true worth of a potato is their fluffy warm texture when boiled. Add drained potatoes, tuna and olives to a bowl, then add dressing ingredients. The salad will be clumpy if mayonnaise alone is added, but with milk it's smooth. Finish with a dash of curry powder.

Ingredients (Serves 4)
3 potatoes
10 green olives
1 can tuna

Dressing
2 Tbsp mayonnaise
1 Tbsp each milk, vinegar
1 tsp olive oil
1/2 tsp curry powder
2 pinches sugar
1 pinch salt
Parsley, salt and pepper, to taste

Crispy Potato Salad

A crunchy, fun dish

For potatoes, white and round types come to mind, but for this salad waxier potatoes have a nice crunchiness that makes them a perfect fit. Peel the potatoes and boil briefly. Drain and cut into bite-size pieces. Soften dried tomatoes by soaking them for 5 minutes in hot water. Drain. Add potatoes, dried tomatoes, anchovies, and parsley, then toss with dressing. The potatoes take on the savory taste of the tomatoes and anchovies.

Ingredients (Serves 4)

3 May Queen potatoes (or russet)
5 slices dried tomatoes
2 anchovies, minced
2 to 3 Tbsp fresh parsley, minced

Dressing

1 Tbsp each vinegar, olive oil
1/2 Tbsp soy sauce
Pinch each sugar, salt
Pepper, to taste

Cilantro Salad
An invigorating aroma!

This is a salad for all the cilantro lovers out there—a mound of energizing green goodness. Cut cilantro into bite-size pieces, dice the tomato, and toss with dressing. The Asian-style dressing, rich in flavor with ginger and onion, complements the cilantro. The flavor soaks in quickly so be sure to add the dressing just before serving.

Ingredients (Serves 2 to 4)
1 bunch cilantro
1 tomato

Dressing
2 Tbsp finely chopped onion, soaked in water and patted dry
Dash each grated garlic, grated ginger
1 Tbsp each: lemon juice, soy sauce, sesame oil
Pinch sugar
Dash Worcestershire sauce

Watercress Salad

The spiciness is irresistible!

I truly love watercress. That crunchy, spicy, unique flavor of watercress is a personal favorite. So here is a salad of just watercress. The stems have a special taste, so only cut off about 1/4" at the roots. Cut into bite-size pieces, put in a bowl and toss with dressing. Watercress almost always plays second-fiddle to meat but it can be a main player on its own.

Ingredients (Serves 2 to 4)
2 bunches watercress

Dressing
Dash grated garlic
1 to 2 Tbsp lemon juice
1 Tbsp each olive oil, vinegar
1 light Tbsp mayonnaise
2 pinches salt
Pinch sugar
Pepper, to taste

Carrot Salad

A nice, crispy, toothsome crunch

Raw carrots are truly sweet and delicious, and so is carrot salad. Slice carrot into rounds on the bias, then julienne. This way it absorbs the flavor and is still crunchy. The sugar and honey bring out the carrot's sweetness. Mix all ingredients and toss with dressing. Eat soon after or set aside, both ways are delicious.

Ingredients (Serves 2 to 4)
1 carrot
10 olives (black, pitted) finely
  chopped

Dressing
1 Tbsp each vinegar, olive oil
1 tsp each: honey, sugar
2 pinches salt

19

Grilled Pepper Marinade
Toss grilled peppers in olive oil

Marinated grilled peppers are deliciously fragrant. Combine marinade ingredients in a bowl and set aside. Cut each pepper into 4 to 6 pieces. Pour oil into heated pan and grill peppers. Add chili pepper and garlic, and grill until lightly browned. Add to a bowl with marinade ingredients and let your refrigerator do the rest.

Ingredients (Serves 4)
1 each green, red and yellow bell pepper
2 cloves garlic
3 red chili peppers (stems and seeds removed)
2 Tbsp olive oil

Marinade
2 Tbsp rice vinegar
1 tsp sugar
1/3 tsp salt
Pepper, to taste

Turnip and Basil Marinade

Turnips invigorated with peppercorns

It's best to leave the skin on turnips when eating them raw. The skin makes it crunchy on the outside, and the contrast with the creamy texture inside is just unbeatable. Add the peppercorns whole for crispness and spicy accent. Multicolored peppercorns add a colorful flair, but using black and white is fine, too.

Ingredients (Serves 4)
1 turnip
15 basil leaves

Marinade
2 Tbsp rice vinegar
Dash grated garlic
1 1/2 Tbsp olive oil
1/2 Tbsp multicolored (or black) peppercorns
1 tsp each sugar and salt

Chinese-style Celery Marinade

Richly refreshing

Munch on a bite of celery and your mouth is filled with freshness. Cut lengthwise into long pieces for satisfying, crunchy bites. Peel celery, mince ginger and add both to a marinade of sesame oil, star anise, and oyster sauce. Add the soft leaves as well. This dish has a rich flavor yet complements a wide variety of meals.

Ingredients (Serves 2 to 4)

2 stalks celery
1/2 nub ginger

Marinade

2 star anise
Dash grated garlic
1 Tbsp each sesame oil, vinegar,
    oyster sauce
1/2 tsp salt
1/2 tsp sugar

Zucchini Marinade

Savory grilled zucchini

I love zucchini. They're juicy like a cucumber yet soft like eggplants. Cut the zucchini in long, thin slices, grill both sides in olive oil, then add the cottage cheese and anchovies. Grill until fragrant, and you'll fall for zucchini all over again. Eat it while it's hot or chill first.

Ingredients (Serves 4)
2 zucchinis
1 Tbsp olive oil

Marinade
2 anchovies, finely chopped
5 Tbsp cottage cheese
Dash grated garlic
Pinch each salt, sugar
Dash each pepper, dried basil

Asparagus with Baby Sardines

Munch on lightly boiled asparagus

Crisp asparagus and crunchy sardines can work as a side dish or a snack. Cut 2/5" (1 cm) off the root end, and peel the skin off the bottom third. Blanch briefly in salted boiling water, drain, and cut in half lengthwise. Broil sardines until browned and crispy, then mix with dressing. Add dressing to asparagus and serve.

Ingredients (Serves 2 to 4)
1 bunch asparagus

Dressing
3 Tbsp baby sardines (*jako*)
Dash grated ginger
1 Tbsp sesame oil
1 Tbsp roasted sesame seeds (white, black)
1 light Tbsp soy sauce
1/2 Tbsp mirin (sweet cooking wine)

Mizuna and **Tofu Salad**

Fresh *mizuna* and creamy tofu

Boiling and stewing *mizuna* is customary, but a fresh salad is a great way to serve this juicy green. Drain excess water from the tofu, then add to a bowl with *mizuna*. Add the dressing and mix while tossing with a spatula. It's important to mix them well since the soft tofu brings out the fresh crunch of the *mizuna*'s. The ginger in the dressing is a nice accent. Finish with a bunch of bonito flakes.

Ingredients (Serves 4)
1 bunch *mizuna* (or sub. arugula)
1 block tofu (soft)
Bonito flakes, to taste

Dressing
Dash grated ginger
1 Tbsp each soy sauce, sesame oil,
    roasted white sesame seeds
Pinch sugar

Turnip Greens and Boiled Egg Salad

Raw greens are delicious!

It's popular to have recipes with boiled turnip greens but raw greens in a salad is mouthwatering. It's soft and savory as soon as you bite into it. Toss the turnip leaves with dressing and then garnish with eggs, anchovies and olives. Don't overcook the eggs—keep the yolk nice and creamy. It's like a second dressing!

Ingredients (Serves 4)

1 bunch turnip greens (*aburana*. Or mustard greens or spinach)
2 boiled eggs (peeled and cut into 8ths)
2 anchovies
Several black pitted olives
Several stuffed green olives

Dressing

Dash grated garlic
1 Tbsp each vinegar, olive oil
2 pinches salt
1 pinch sugar
Pepper, to taste

Rapini and Scallop Salad

Boil lightly

Rapini are at their finest for only a short period in the spring. They have a refreshing bitterness. Avoid overcooking, since the stems are best when crunchy. Mix the canned scallops along with the canning liquid into the rapini and combine with the mustard-flavored dressing. The sweetness of the scallops, the bitterness of the rapini and the spicy mustard balanced with mayonnaise makes for a very spring-y dish.

Ingredients (Serves 2 to 4)
1 bunch rapini (broccoli raab)
1 can scallops

Dressing
Dash grated ginger
1 Tbsp mayonnaise
1/2 tsp yellow mustard
Dash each sesame oil, soy sauce

String Bean and Tomato Salad

String beans have a sweet crunch, and the dressing is a fresh delight

You'll want to keep that crispiness, so simply blanch the beans for 30 seconds. Drain and cut in half, and arrange on a plate. Combine ingredients for dressing, then add shallots and tomatoes. Add dressing on top of the beans. It's okay to mix and toss everything together, but the red and green look beautiful when done up neatly. The shallots are a little spicy. They're related to leeks.

Ingredients (Serves 2 to 4)
1 bag string beans
1/2 tomato, diced into 1/4" cubes
2 shallots, minced

Dressing
Dash grated garlic
1 Tbsp each olive oil, vinegar
2 pinches salt
Dash sugar
Pepper, to taste

Endive and Blue Cheese Salad

A grown-up salad best complemented by white wine

Once you try endives you won't be able to get enough of that crunch and that slightly bitter taste. The richness of the blue cheese and sweet and sour of the apple balance out perfectly. First, peel the leaves off the endive one by one. Slice the apple into 8ths, then smaller pieces, then mix into dressing. Crumble blue cheese and add to dressing. Place endive leaves on plate and coat with dressing, then garnish with walnuts. This salad is a time-honored favorite.

Ingredients (Serves 4)
1 endive
1/2 apple
1 3/4 oz (50g) blue cheese
    (Gorgonzola or Roquefort)
Dry roasted walnuts, to taste

Dressing
1 Tbsp each mayonnaise, milk
1/2 Tbsp olive oil
1 pinch salt

Simply Chic

Here are some simple-yet-chic side dishes designed to show the true power of vegetables—the sweetness, the bitterness, even the crunch. You don't need to add much to these dishes since you want the veggies' natural flavor to shine through.
Simplicity is very chic.

Yam Steak

Grilled to perfection

Recipe on page 50

A grilled yam seasoned with salt and pepper. No fancy ingredients, but that's the way to do it if you want the perfect yam steak.

Endive Sauté
Savory grilled goodness

Recipe on page 50

The bitterness of endives is an acquired taste. Sautéing enhances the flavor, and the oil gives it depth. The light, creamy garlic sauce unleashes the pure taste of the vegetable.

Cabbage in Sesame Oil

A sweet aroma to awaken the senses

Recipe on page 50

Big chunks of cabbage flavored with salt and oyster sauce then finished with a drizzle of sesame oil. The oils lock in the savory flavors and the fresh cabbage gives a satisfying crunch.

Fried Sweet Potato

Golden sweetness, served warm

Recipe on page 51

Fry the potato slowly and steadily, until it's nice and soft on the inside. The crispy outside and fluffy inside will make your mouth water.

Green Onion Omelette

A dose of sweet green onion

Recipe on page 51

Take a panful of sautéed green onion and mix it with grated ginger and scrambled egg for a delicious meal. Rice is the perfect side dish.

Grilled Leek

The perfect combination of sweet and flavorful

Recipe on page 51

The appeal of a grilled leek lies in the crispy outside and soft inside. Onions are often used to sweeten or spice up a dish, but it's taking the leading role this time, so dig in!

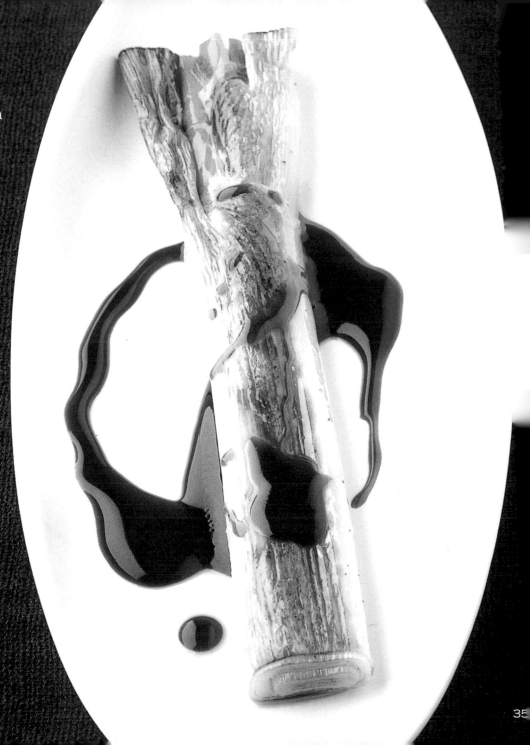

Daikon with Yuzu

The skin gives a good crunchiness

Recipe on page 51

Since the texture as well as the taste of a vegetable changes depending on how it's cut, deciding which way to slice it is part of the fun in cooking. Even with daikon—along the grain, against the grain, thin or thick—the taste changes. For this meal, use thick slices for a toothsome morsel.

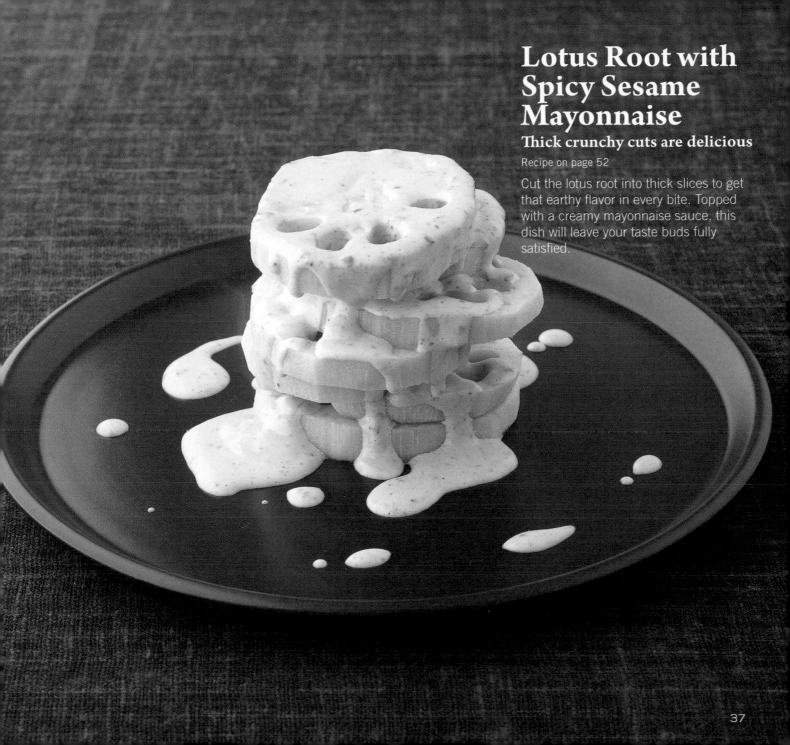

Lotus Root with Spicy Sesame Mayonnaise

Thick crunchy cuts are delicious

Recipe on page 52

Cut the lotus root into thick slices to get that earthy flavor in every bite. Topped with a creamy mayonnaise sauce, this dish will leave your taste buds fully satisfied.

Cucumber and Garlic Stir-Fry

Fragrant, salty and sweet

Recipe on page 52

The fresh juiciness of sautéed cucumbers will flood your taste buds. Garlic, salt and oil give it the perfect flavor. The key is to be quick when frying.

Spicy Pickles
Not just spicy!

Recipe on page 52

Pounded and shredded spicy pickled cucumbers. Pounding first helps the cucumber soak in more flavor while keeping them perfectly crunchy. These are so good, they'll be gone before you know it.

Kabocha Sauté with Honey Sauce

A sweet sauce is the perfect treat

Recipe on page 52

Sweet honey and salty butter are a heavenly complement to perfectly grilled *kabocha*. If the butter burns the flavors go out the window, so gently heat just until melted.

Simmered *Kabocha*

Hefty pieces

Recipe on page 52

Cut into large chunks and simmer to perfection. Leave the skin on for extra flavor. The sunny explosion of sweet *kabocha* is a delight.

Grilled *Maitake* with Cheese

Easy to make in a toaster oven!

Recipe on page 53

Whenever I eat mushrooms, I always wonder where the juicy goodness comes from. Before you broil these *maitake*, make sure you add pepper and olive oil. It can't be beat!

Shiitake Stir-fry Donburi

Delicious smell, delicious taste

Recipe on page 53

It's the garlic, ginger, soy sauce, oyster sauce and prickly ash *tsukudani* that really push this rice bowl over the top. This tantalizing mushroom medley on rice will leave you wanting more!

Shiitake and Red Miso Stir-fry

A thick, sweet and spicy sauce

Recipe on page 53

Sweet miso is the perfect dressing to draw out the full flavors of the
fragrant shiitake mushroom. The natural juiciness of the mushrooms
add to the dish, so be sure to buy nice, fat shiitake.

41

Garlic Chive Stir-fry

A powerful punch

Recipe on page 53

A mound of chives and a heap of garlic sautéed to perfection.
Put the heat on high and mix it up. Easy to make and quick
to finish up, this is a one-dish pleasure.

Chives and Eggs
Sunny goodness in every bite
Recipe on page 53

An easy-to-make dish of chives and eggs
simmered in a noodle soup base. Of course
you can always add this to a bowl of rice
if you have a hearty appetite.

Kinpira-style *Udo*

Savor the unique texture

Recipe on page 54

The taste will change depending how the *udo* is sliced. When it's cut thinly, it has a slick and crunchy mouthfeel. *Udo* is great with a little oil, and chili pepper gives it a very nice kick.

Salted Kinpira-style Celery

A salty crunch

Recipe on page 54

A perfect recipe to show off celery's fragrance and color. A soy- and mirin-based kinpira is customary but this salt kinpira is also a great dish. It's a simple dish packed with a lot of flavor.

Kinpira-style Burdock
The king of kinpira
Recipe on page 54

This is a dish Japan can pride itself on.
Be sure not to overdo it with the heat—a quick
sauté is best. The secret to a perfect kinpira
lies in the oil and cooked soy sauce. Scrub the
root with a hard brush to remove any dirt.

Salted *Komatsuna*

Garlic plays an important role

Recipe on page 55

Add an ample amount of sugar and salt to the rich *komatsuna*—and don't forget the garlic! You can toss everything with your hands for faster preparation.

Potato Namul

Waxy potato a must!

Recipe on page 55

Cut potato into long, thin sticks, and boil through. The crunch will mesmerize your mouth and leave your senses satisfied.

Seasoned Parsley

An alluring bitterness

Recipe on page 55

Parsley has the refreshing flavor of spring. Just add a drop of soy sauce to bring out the rich, slightly bitter flavors.

Spicy Cauliflower

Enhanced by curry

Recipe on page 55

Cauliflower has a unique sweetness. Add some curry powder and spice for a mouthwatering delight.

Spinach *Ohitashi*

A must-have recipe!

Recipe on page 49

Boil the leaves first—that's the best way. Boil until dark green to bring out the natural sweetness. It's the simplicity of this dish that makes it so special.

Spinach *Ohitashi*

Rinse well after boiling

Photo page 48

Ingredients (Serves 2 to 4)
1 bunch spinach
Handful bonito flakes
Soy sauce, to taste

Instructions
1. Bring salted water to a boil and add spinach, leaves first, and let boil for 15 to 20 seconds. Remove spinach and shock in ice water. Drain, and squeeze out any excess water and cut into 2" (5 cm) pieces.
2. Serve on a dish with a drizzle of soy sauce and bonito flakes on top.

1. Boiling the spinach quickly is key. I put the spinach in leaves first, and boil until they turn dark green. Use a large pot so the water doesn't cool when you add the spinach.

2. After boiling for 15 seconds, remove from the water and place in a bowl.

3. Spinach tends to have a filmy layer after boiling, so rinse thoroughly. Winter spinach has a bitterness that gives flavor but it's not always wanted.

4. Squeeze the spinach well to drain excess water. Be careful not to wring it as this will make the spinach stringy.

Yam Steak

Cover and fry

Photo page 30

Ingredients (Serves 2 to 4)

4" (10 cm) yam
1/2 Tbsp vegetable oil
Salt and pepper, to taste

Instructions

1. Peel yam and cut in half.
2. Add oil to a heated pan, add yam and cover with lid. Cook over low heat until browned, then turn over. Season with pepper. Remove from heat once a skewer can be easily inserted into yam.
3. Garnish with salt and serve.

Endive Sauté

Savory garlic

Photo page 31

Ingredients (Serves 2)

2 endives
1 clove garlic
1 Tbsp olive oil
1 Tbsp white wine
1/2 C fresh cream
Salt and pepper, to taste

Instructions

1. Cut endives in half lengthwise. Finely chop garlic.
2. Add oil to heated pan. Add endives and season with salt and pepper. Cook on high heat until browned, then turn over. Add garlic to open area of pan and sauté.
3. When both sides of endives are browned, at white wine and sauté. Add fresh cream and simmer over medium heat. When cream thickens, season with salt. Sprinkle with pepper and serve.

Cabbage in Sesame Oil

Lots of sesame flavor

Photo page 32

Ingredients (Serves 4)

1/4 head cabbage
1/2 nub ginger
A [1/2 tsp oyster sauce
  [Pinch each salt, sugar
3 to 4 Tbsp sesame oil
1/2 Tbsp each ground sesame seeds (black or white)

Instructions

1. Cut cabbage into bite-size pieces and mince ginger. Add cabbage, ginger and mixture A to a bowl and stir. Let sit for about 5 minutes, then place on a dish.
2. Add sesame oil to heated pan, and heat briefly. Pour hot oil over cabbage, then sprinkle with ground sesame seeds.

Fried Sweet Potato

Cover and cook on low, then finish with high heat

Photo page 33

Ingredients (Serves 2 to 4)

1 medium sweet potato
Dash each salt, brown sugar
Oil, for frying

Instructions

1. Cut unpeeled sweet potato in half, then quarter lengthwise. Soak in salted water for 3 minutes.
2. Heat 1 1/4" (3 cm) oil over medium heat. Drain potato, pat dry and add to oil. When oil starts to bubble, lower heat, cover with lid, and cook slowly until a skewer can be easily inserted. Then turn heat to high and brown on both sides.
3. Remove from pan and garnish with salt and sugar.

Note

When frying, start with the skin side up. If you fry the skin first, it could burn.

Green Onion Omelet

Add sugar for a little sweetness

Photo page 34

Ingredients (Serves 3)

2 stalks green onion (or leeks)
1 clove garlic
1 Tbsp sesame oil
1 Tbsp sake
1 tsp soy sauce
1/2 tsp mirin (sweet cooking wine)
A ⎡ 3 eggs
⎜ 2 pinches sugar
⎣ Pinch salt
1/2 Tbsp vegetable oil

Instructions

1. Slice green onions on the bias and mince ginger. Add mixture A to a bowl and stir thoroughly.
2. Add sesame oil to a heated pan. Sauté garlic on low heat until fragrant. Add green onions and cook over medium heat. When onion is tender, add sake and stir-fry. When the alcohol has burned off, add soy sauce and mirin, then stir-fry. Remove from heat and set aside.
3. Wipe pan clean, then add oil and mixture A. Cook over medium heat. Before the egg cooks through, add ingredients from step 2 to egg mixture and stir until it fills pan evenly. Cook until both sides are done. Fold in half and serve.

Grilled Leek

Just cook on low

Photo page 35

Ingredients (Serves 2)

1 leek (or green onion)
1/2 Tbsp sesame oil
Dash salt
Oyster sauce, to taste

Instructions

1. Cut leek in half lengthwise. Add oil to heated pan. Add leek, sprinkle with salt and fry over medium heat. Transfer to a dish. Finish with oyster sauce and serve.

Daikon with Yuzu

Soak longer for a stronger flavor

Photo page 36

Ingredients (Serves 4)

5" (12 cm) daikon
1 x 1" piece yuzu (or lemon) peel
1 red chili pepper
A ⎡ 1/4 C water
⎜ 1 1/2 tsp salt
⎜ 1 tsp sake
⎣ Dash sugar

Instructions

1. Leave skin on daikon and cut in half lengthwise, then slice into bars 2/3" (1 1/2 cm) wide. Julienne yuzu peel and remove stem and seeds of chili pepper.
2. Add mixture A to bowl and mix with daikon, yuzu and chili pepper. Marinate in refrigerator for at least 1 hour.

Lotus Root with Spicy Sesame Mayonnaise

3 M's—mayo, miso, and milk

Photo page 37

Ingredients (Serves 2 to 4)

6 1/2 oz (180 g) lotus root (*renkon*)

A ⎰ 2 Tbsp each mayonnaise, milk
⎱ 1 Tbsp ground white sesame seeds
1 tsp miso
1 tsp Japanese (or hot English) mustard
1/2 tsp sugar

Instructions

1. Peel lotus root and cut into rounds 1/4" (7 mm) thick. Soak in vinegared water for about 3 minutes. Bring salted water to a boil and add drained lotus root. Cook until tender.
2. Transfer lotus root to a plate and garnish with mixture A.

Cucumber and Garlic Stir-fry

Peel the skin so the flavor soaks in

Photo page 38

Ingredients (Serves 4)

3 cucumbers
1 clove garlic
1 chili pepper
1 Tbsp sesame oil
1 Tbsp sake
Salt, to taste

Instructions

1. Peel cucumbers and cut into bite-size wedges. Finely chop garlic. Remove stem and seeds from chili pepper.
2. Add oil to heated pan and sauté garlic on low heat until fragrant. Add chili pepper and cucumbers and sauté until cucumbers soften. Add sake and sauté. When alcohol burns off, season with salt.

Spicy Pickles

Pound those cukes!

Photo page 38

Ingredients (Serves 4)

4 cucumbers

A ⎰ 1/2 nub ginger, grated
Dash grated garlic
1 Tbsp sesame oil
1/2 Tbsp roasted white sesame seeds
1 tsp of each: Doubanjiang (Chinese chili paste), sugar, oyster sauce, sake, soy sauce, salt

Instructions

1. Pound cucumbers with a rolling pin to tenderize.
2. Add mixture A to a bowl and stir thoroughly. Add cucumbers and mix. Cover with plastic wrap and refrigerate for at least 10 minutes.

Kabocha Sauté with Honey Sauce

Cover when frying

Photo page 39

Ingredients (Serves 2)

1/8 *kabocha* (Japanese pumpkin. Or sub. pumpkin)
1 Tbsp vegetable oil

A ⎰ 1 Tbsp butter
1 tsp honey
Pinch salt

Instructions

1. Remove seeds from *kabocha* with a spoon. Cut into 1/5" (5 mm) wide slices. Add oil to a heated pan. Add half of *kabocha* slices, cover with a lid and cook over medium heat. Remove from heat when both sides are browned and a skewer can be easily inserted. Repeat with remaining portion of *kabocha*.
2. Add mixture A to a small pan and heat briefly. Stir and remove from heat.
3. Serve on dish with butter on top.

Simmered *Kabocha*

Don't let it boil over!

Photo page 39

Ingredients (Serves 4)

1/4 *kabocha* (Japanese pumpkin)

A ⎰ 1 1/2 C water
1 Tbsp each sake, mirin (sweet cooking wine)
1 1/2 Tbsp soy sauce
Pinch salt

Instructions

1. Remove seeds from *kabocha*. Cut into bite-size chunks.
2. Add mixture A to a pot. Add *kabocha* skin-side down and cover with a lid. Simmer on medium-low heat for 20 minutes.

Grilled *Maitake* with Cheese

Don't forget to add the olive oil

Photo page 40

Ingredients (Serves 4)

1 pack *maitake* (sheep's head) mushroom
1/2 Tbsp olive oil
1 pinch salt
Dash each black pepper, dried basil
3 to 4 Tbsp shredded cheese

Instructions

1. Place mushrooms on a sheet of aluminum foil. Sprinkle olive oil, salt, pepper, basil and cheese on top.
2. Broil until cheese is golden brown.

Shiitake Stir-fry Donburi

Careful—overcooked mushrooms get watery

Photo page 40

Ingredients (Serves 2)

4 to 5 shiitake mushrooms
1/2 nub ginger
1/2 clove garlic
1/2 Tbsp sesame oil
2 Tbsp sake
A ⌈ 1 tsp soy sauce
⎜ 1/2 oyster sauce
⌊ Pinch sugar
2 servings white rice
Tsukudani, to taste (see Reference Guide)
Japanese pickles, to taste

Instructions

1. Cut stems off mushrooms, then quarter lengthwise. Mince garlic and ginger. Add mixture A to a bowl and stir.
2. Add oil to heated pan. Sauté ginger and garlic over medium heat until fragrant, then add mushrooms. Cook over high heat until mushrooms are tender. Add sake and stir-fry. Turn off heat and add mixture A, stirring quickly to coat.
3. Serve rice in bowls and top with ingredients from step 2. Garnish with pickles and *tsukudani* vegetables.

Shiitake and Red Miso Stir-fry

The chili peppers give it a kick!

Photo page 41

Ingredients (Serves 2 to 4)

5 to 6 shiitake mushrooms
2 chili peppers
1 Tbsp sesame oil
A ⌈ 1 Tbsp sake
⎜ 1/2 Tbsp of each red miso, mirin
⎜ (sweet cooking wine)
⌊ 1 Tbsp soy sauce

Instructions

1. Cut stems off mushrooms, then halve lengthwise. Remove stems and seeds of chili peppers and tear into pieces. Add mixture A to a bowl and set aside.
2. Add oil to a heated pan. Add chili peppers and mushrooms and stir-fry over medium heat. When the mushrooms are tender add mixture A and stir over high heat.

Garlic Chive Stir-fry

Use lots of pepper

Photo page 42

Ingredients (Serves 2)

2 bunches garlic chives
2 to 3 cloves garlic
1 Tbsp sesame oil
Salt and pepper, to taste

Instructions

1. Cut chives into 2" (5 mm) pieces. Mince garlic.
2. Add sesame oil to heated pan. Sauté garlic over low heat until fragrant. Add chives and stir-fry until tender. Season with salt, then finish with pepper and serve.

Chives and Eggs

When the soup boils, add the chives

Photo page 43

Ingredients (Serves 2)

1 bunch garlic chives
2 eggs
1/4 C diluted noodle sauce (*men tsuyu*. See Reference Guide)

Instructions

1. Cut the chives into 2" (5 cm) pieces.
2. Add noodle sauce to a pan and bring to a boil. Add chives and eggs to pan and cover with lid. Simmer on medium-low heat until the eggs are done to your liking.

Kinpira-style *Udo*

Add oil to keep it from burning!

Photo page 44

Ingredients (Serves 2)

1/2 stalk *udo* (Aralia cordata.
   Or sub asparagus or fennel)
1 Tbsp sesame oil
1 Tbsp mirin (sweet cooking wine)
1 light Tbsp soy sauce
2 chili peppers
1 Tbsp roasted white sesame seeds

Instructions

1. Peel tough skin off *udo* then halve
   lengthwise. Cut slices lengthwise again
   into thin bars. If bitter, soak in vinegared
   water for 3 minutes. Remove stem and
   seeds of chili peppers and mince.
2. Add sesame oil to a heated pan. Add
   udo and stir-fry over high heat until
   tender on both sides and the surface is
   transparent. Add mirin and soy sauce,
   then stir-fry. Add chili pepper and
   sesame seeds, then mix.

Salted Kinpira-style Celery

Just a quick sauté to complete

Photo page 44

Ingredients (Serve 2 to 4)

2 stalks celery
2 chili peppers
1 Tbsp sesame oil
1 Tbsp mirin (sweet cooking wine)
Dash salt

Instructions

1. Peel celery and cut into 2" (5 cm)
   pieces, then cut finely lengthwise.
   Shred leaves. Remove stem and seeds
   of chili peppers.
2. Add sesame oil to a heated pan. Add
   celery and stir-fry over high heat until
   tender. Add the chili pepper and stir-
   fry. Add mirin and salt, and stir well.
   Add celery leaves and stir briefly.

Kinpira-style Burdock

High heat is key

Photo page 45

Ingredients (Serves 4)

1 burdock root (or salsify)
1 carrot
1 Tbsp sesame oil
1 Tbsp + 1 tsp mirin
   (sweet cooking wine)
1 light Tbsp soy sauce
2 Tbsp roasted black sesame seeds
Cayenne pepper, to taste

Instructions

1. Scrub burdock while rinsing with water.
   Thinly shave off slices with a peeler
   and soak in vinegared water for about 3
   minutes. Peel carrot, then thinly shave
   with a peeler.
2. Add sesame oil to heated pan. Remove
   burdock from water, pat dry and add
   to pan. Add carrots and cook over high
   heat until tender. Add mirin and soy
   sauce and stir-fry. Once seasonings are
   evenly distributed, add sesame seeds
   and stir. Serve on dishes and finish
   with cayenne pepper.

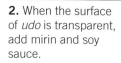

1. Chop thinly to keep that toothsome texture.

2. When the surface of *udo* is transparent, add mirin and soy sauce.

3. When the seasonings are evenly distributed, add chili pepper and sesame seeds. Give it a stir and it's finished!

Salted *Komatsuna*

Toss and serve!

Photo page 46

Ingredients (Serves 2)

1/2 bunch *komatsuna* (or sub mustard
greens, spinach or bok choy)

A
- Dash grated garlic
- 3 to 4 Tbsp roasted white sesame seeds
- 1 Tbsp sesame oil
- A few pinches each salt, sugar

Instructions

1. Boil komatsuna in salted water. Drain
   in a colander and cool. Remove and
   squeeze out excess water. Cut into 2"
   (5 cm) long pieces.
2. In a bowl add mixture A and mix well.
   Add *komatsuna* and toss.

Note

**Don't rinse *komatsuna* after boiling.
The residual heat will continue cooking
the vegetable while in the colander, so
don't over-boil.
Mix with dressing right before serving.
It will get watery if it sits for too long.**

Potato Namul

A little spice!

Photo page 46

Ingredients (Serves 2 to 4)

2 May Queen potatoes (sub Red or
fingerling or Yukon)

A
- Dash grated garlic
- 2 Tbsp ground white sesame
- 1 Tbsp sesame oil
- 2 pinches salt
- Pinch sugar

Cayenne pepper to taste

Instructions

1. Cut potatoes lengthwise into thin slices
   and soak in water for 3 minutes. In a
   pot, bring salted water to a boil and
   add potatoes. When the surfaces of
   the potatoes are transparent remove
   from water.
2. In a bowl combine mixture A. Add
   potatoes and toss. Finish with cayenne
   pepper.

Seasoned Parsley

**Just a quick swish through
boiling water!**

Photo page 47

Ingredients (Serves 2 to 4)

1 bunch parsley

A
- 1 Tbsp each sesame oil, ground black sesame seeds
- 2 pinches each salt, sugar
- Dash soy sauce

Instructions

1. Briefly boil parsley in salted water.
   Remove and dry, then cut into 2"
   (5 cm) pieces.
2. In a bowl, combine mixture A and stir.
   Add parsley and toss to coat.

Spicy Cauliflower

**A little boiling leaves a lot of
crunch**

Photo page 47

Ingredients (Serves 4)

1 head of cauliflower

A
- 1 Tbsp sesame oil
- 1 tsp curry powder
- 1/2 to 1 tsp gochujang (Korean hot pepper paste)
- 2 pinches each sugar, salt

Instructions

1. Cut the cauliflower into bite-size pieces
   and boil in salted water.
2. In a bowl, combine mixture A and stir.
   Add cauliflower and toss to coat.

Grilled Vegetables

How can such simply prepared veggies be so good?

Recipe page 58

Summer vegetables are soaked in sunlight. Line your favorite vegetables on the grill, drizzle with olive oil and some salt, then grill away! Grilling concentrates the veggies' natural sweetness. You'll find whole new layers of flavors to appreciate. These recipes will fill you with energy!

Bountiful Main Dishes

It's not just about eating healthy. The grand flavors of vegetables make them a favorite food. Vegetable dishes so succulent and delicious you won't even need any sides. Make room for the new leader—vegetables.

Ginger Eggplant

A hearty crunch and light flavor

Recipe page 59

Ginger, eggplant and oil—a trio made in heaven. The oil gives a nice rich taste while the ginger adds some zest. A light and irresistible recipe you won't forget.

Grilled Vegetables

Two trays in the oven for grilled goodness!

Photo page 56

Ingredients (Serves 4)

2 potatoes
1/8 *kabocha* (or sub acorn squash)
1 each red, yellow bell pepper
1 zucchini
2 tomato
1 clove garlic
Olive oil, as needed
Salt and pepper, to taste

Cheese Sauce

3 1/2 Tbsp (50 g) cream cheese
3 anchovies
1 clove garlic
1 Tbsp olive oil
1 Tbsp white wine
A ⌈ 1 C fresh cream
  | 1/2 C milk
  ⌊ 1/2 tsp dried basil
Salt and pepper, to taste

Instructions

1. Peel potatoes and slice into 2/5" (1 cm) thick rounds. Soak in water for 3 minutes. Remove seeds from *kabocha*, and cut into 1" thick slices. Quarter bell peppers lengthwise. Slice zucchini lengthwise into 1/5" (5 mm) thick strips. Leave skin on garlic and slice in half. Leave tomatoes whole.
2. Prepare two baking sheets and grease with a small amount of olive oil. On one sheet, line up potato and *kabocha* slices. Add remaining vegetables to the second sheet. Douse vegetables with olive oil and add salt and pepper.
3. Heat oven to 390°F (200°C) and insert pan with potatoes. Cook for 12 minutes, then increase heat to 480°F (250°C) and insert pan with other vegetables. Cook for 5 minutes.
4. While vegetables are cooking, make the cheese sauce: cut cream cheese into 2/5" (1 cm) thick blocks or crumble by hand. Finely chop anchovies. Leave skin on garlic and cut in half, then mince.
5. Add oil to a small heated pan. Sauté garlic until fragrant then add anchovies and stir. Add white wine and stir-fry. Add mixture A and cheese, stir until cheese is melted and simmer over low heat. Season with salt and pepper.
6. Serve vegetables with sauce on side.

Ginger Eggplant

A gathering of flavorful goodness

Photo page 57

Ingredients (Serves 4)

5 eggplants (the small Japanese or
    Italian kind)
1 *myoga* ginger bud (or sub. ginger root,
    peeled)
10 shiso leaves (or sub. basil or mint)
1 pack daikon sprouts (*kaiware*)
1 Tbsp dried shrimp
2 Tbsp hot water

A ⎡ 1/2 nub ginger, grated
  ⎢ 1 1/2 Tbsp soy sauce
  ⎢ 1 Tbsp each mirin (sweet cooking
  ⎣   wine), sesame oil

Roasted sesame seeds (white, black)
    and cayenne pepper, to taste
Oil, for frying

Instructions

1. Cut eggplant into quarters lengthwise and soak in heavily salted water for 3 minutes. Slice *myoga* ginger bud on the bias and mince shiso. Cut stems off daikon sprouts. Soak shrimp in warm water.
2. Add mixture A to the bowl with shrimp. Stir and set aside.
3. Add 3/4" (2 cm) oil to heated pan. Pat eggplant dry and add 4 slices skin-side up. Fry over high heat until browned then turn over and cook skin side briefly. Remove from oil and add to ingredients from step 2. Marinate for at least 5 minutes.
4. Place eggplants on plate and garnish with ginger, shiso, and sprouts. Finish with roasted sesame seeds and cayenne pepper.

Potato Gratin
Hearty hunks of tasty 'taters

Recipe page 62

A simple potato gratin with thick pieces of potato that will warm you to the bone. Anchovies give it a salty kick and the garlic is the perfect sauce seasoning. Bite into the sweet taste of potato.

Tomato Stew

The proud taste of turnip and potato

Recipe page 63

Potatoes in a tomato stew are great, but a grainy texture is not. Be sure to boil the potatoes separately and give it enough time to get the texture just right.

Potato Gratin

Use coarse-ground pepper

Photo page 60

Ingredients (Serves 4)

3 to 4 potatoes
3 anchovies
1 clove garlic
1 Tbsp olive oil
1 Tbsp white wine
4/5 C (200 ml) fresh cream
Salt and pepper, to taste
3/4 C shredded mozzarella cheese

Instructions

1. Peel potatoes and cut into 2/5" (1 cm) thick rounds. Add potatoes to a bowl with water and soak for 3 minutes, then boil potatoes in a pot until a skewer can be easily inserted (about 5 minutes). Remove from heat and drain in a colander.
2. Make the sauce: finely chop anchovies and garlic. Add oil to heated pan and sauté garlic until fragrant. Add anchovies and sauté briefly, then add white wine and stir-fry. Add fresh cream, reduce heat to low, and stir. Continue to simmer until it develops a creamy texture. Season with salt and pepper.
3. Rinse an oven-safe dish with water, then add 1/3 of cream sauce. Line half the potatoes on top, then cover with half of the mozzarella cheese. Add another 1/3 of cream sauce. Add the second half of the potatoes then cover with remaining cheese and the final 1/3 of the sauce. Season with plenty of pepper and cook in the oven on 475°F (250°C) for 15 minutes.

Tomato Stew
Boil the potatoes separately and add last

Photo page 61

Ingredients (Serves 4)

2 Red (or Yukon) potatoes
1 turnip
2 cloves garlic
8 oz (225 g) short-neck clams
  (canned)
1 Tbsp olive oil
1 Tbsp white wine

A
- 1 14 oz (400 g) can whole tomatoes
- 1 C water
- 1 bay leaf
- 1/2 tsp oregano
- Dash curry powder

Salt and pepper, to taste
10 basil leaves (fresh)
Plain yogurt, as needed

Instructions

1. Peel potatoes and cut into bite-size pieces. Boil until tender. Remove from heat and drain.
2. Remove leaves from turnip, then peel and cut into 4 to 6 evenly-sized pieces. Halve garlic and crush with flat of knife.
3. Add olive oil to heated pan. Sauté garlic on low heat until fragrant. Add clams and sauté over high heat. Once the clams are evenly coated with oil, add turnip and stir. Once turnips are coated in oil, add white wine and stir-fry. Add mixture A and simmer on low for 7 to 8 minutes.
4. When turnips are tender, add potatoes. Season with salt and pepper. Add basil and remove pan from heat. Serve and finish with salt, pepper and yogurt

Vegetable Pizza

A mound of vegetables and a delicious, easy sauce

Recipe on page 67

A satisfying pizza with red, yellow and green bell peppers, and zucchini complemented with an easy tomato purée sauce. Finish with some herbs and spices for the perfect bite.

Garlic and Anchovy Pizza

Arugula and garlic give an appealing, balanced flavor

Recipe on page 67

Arugula is a unique green. It's fragrant like sesame and has a sharp taste. Add that to a crispy pizza with anchovies and garlic and you've got one great dish.

1 2 3 4

5 6 7 8

Pizza Dough

Ingredients
(yields six 4 x 8" crusts)
1 1/2 C (200 g) bread flour
2 pinches each salt, sugar
2 to 3 tsp olive oil
2/5 C lukewarm water

Instructions
1. In a bowl, combine flour, oil, salt and sugar (photo 1).
2. Add a little water at a time. Let water soak in and knead with your hands to mix (photos 2, 3). Continue to knead and fold until the dough no longer sticks to your hands (photo 4). When the surface of the dough ball is smooth (photo 5), wrap in plastic film and set aside for 10 minutes.
3. Split dough into 6 parts. Spread flour over flat surface and use a rolling pin to roll dough into thin crusts (photos 6, 7, 8). Poke holes in dough with a fork.

Vegetable Pizza

Nutmeg is the secret ingredient!

Photo page 64

Ingredients (Serves 3)

3 pizza dough crusts
1 zucchini
1 each red, yellow bell pepper
1/2 green bell pepper

A ⎧ dash grated garlic
⎪ 1/2 C tomato puree
⎪ 1 Tbsp olive oil
⎨ 1 heaping Tbsp of each: oregano,
⎪   dried basil
⎪ 1/2 tsp each nutmeg, chili powder
⎩ 3 pinches salt

1/2 C cheese
Olive oil and pepper, to taste

Instructions

1. Cut zucchini into 1/8" (3 mm) thick rounds. Remove stem and seeds from bell peppers and cut into thin rings. Combine mixture A in a bowl.
2. Make one pizza at a time. Spread sauce on dough in circular motion. Lay the zucchini and bell pepper slices on top. Add cheese and olive oil. Cook in oven at 475°F (250°C) for 3 to 7 minutes, or until cheese is browned (each oven is different—check repeatedly until done). Make remaining two pizzas in the same manner.

Garlic and Anchovy Pizza

Add lots of arugula

Photo page 65

Ingredients (Serves 3)

3 pizza dough crusts
1 bunch arugula
1 clove garlic
3 anchovies
1/2 C shredded mozzarella cheese
Olive oil, pepper and grated Parmesan
    cheese, to taste

Instructions

1. Cut root ends off arugula. Thinly slice garlic and remove any green cores. Finely chop anchovies.
2. Make one pizza at a time. Dress with garlic and anchovies, then drizzle with olive oil. Add pepper and mozzarella cheese.
3. Cook in oven at 475°F (250°C) for 3 to 7 minutes, or until cheese is browned (each oven is different—check repeatedly until done). Remove from oven and garnish with arugula, olive oil and pepper. Finish with parmesan cheese. Make remaining two pizzas in the same manner.

1

2

3

Steamed Vegetable Dumplings

Juicy vegetables wrapped in a soft shell

Recipe on page 70

Succulent vegetables wrapped in homemade dough
and served in a warm vegetable broth.
A mouth-watering dish of juicy
vegetables and smooth,
chewy dumpling skins.

Vegetable Tacos
Use spicy beans instead of salsa

Recipe on page 71

Load on the toppings for a colorful and hearty bite! Add some lettuce for crunch, avocado for sweetness and finish with some spicy beans. You won't easily forget the explosion of flavor.

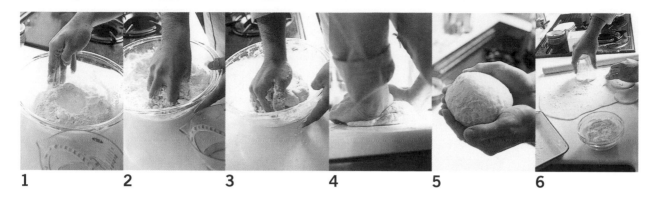

1 **2** **3** **4** **5** **6**

Steamed Vegetable Dumplings

Knead the dough thoroughly

Photo page 68

7 **8** **9**

Ingredients (Serves 4)

2 1/2 C bread flour
1 to 1 1/5C (250 to 300 ml) lukewarm water

Filling

1 oz (30 g) Sichuan vegetable (*zha cai*)
1/4 head (300 g) Napa cabbage
1 bunch garlic chives
1/2 nub ginger
2 Tbsp potato (or corn) starch

A ⌈ 1/2 tsp each sake, sesame oil
  │ 1/2 tsp salt
  │ Pinch sugar
  │ Dash soy sauce
  └ Pepper, to taste

Dipping Sauce

1/2 bunching onion (or leek)

B ⌈ dash grated garlic
  │ 1/4 C soy sauce
  │ 1 to 2 Tbsp sesame oil
  │ 1 Tbsp roasted white sesame
  │   seeds
  │ 1/2 tsp Doubanjiang (Chinese
  │   chili paste)
  └ Rice vinegar, to taste

Instructions

1. Make dumpling wrappers: add flour to a bowl and make an indent in the middle. Add water a little at a time as you mix by hand (photos 1, 2). Once water is mixed in, knead forcefully (photo 3). Once the dough stops sticking to your hands, form into a ball, dust work surface and fold and knead dough (photo 4). When the surface of the dough is smooth (photo 5), wrap in plastic film and set aside for 10 minutes.

2. Make filling: finely chop Sichuan vegetable after rinsing thoroughly. Soak in water for 10 minutes, then dry. Finely chop chives and cabbage. Julienne ginger.

3. In a bowl, add ingredients from step 2, plus potato starch, and mix. When all ingredients are covered with starch, add mixture A and stir.

4. Dust work surface with flour and separate dough into 2 to 3 pieces. Use a rolling pin and work dough until it is 1/10" (2 mm) thick. Use a cup or circular object to cut dumpling pieces from dough (photo 6). Sprinkle rounds with flour.

5. Put a spoonful of filling into the middle of each dumpling wrapper and fold to close. Pinch edges of dumplings to seal (photos 7, 8, 9).

6. Add water to a pot and bring to a boil over high heat. Separate dumplings into 2 batches and put first batch in water. After dumplings rise to top of pot, continue to boil for 1 minute, then remove from water. Break a dumpling in half and check if filling is cooked to your liking. Serve on plates.

7. Combine mixture B. Finely chop bunching onions and add to dipping sauce. Serve alongside dumplings.

1   2   3   4   5   6

Vegetable Tacos

Dry the vegetables well!

Photo page 69

Ingredients (Serves 4)

Tortillas

A ⎡ 1 2/3 C pastry flour
  ⎢ 1 tsp baking powder
  ⎣ 1 pinch each salt, sugar
1 1/4 C water
Vegetable oil, as needed

Chili Filling

1 can soy (or black) beans
1 clove garlic
1 Tbsp olive oil
1 Tbsp white wine

B ⎡ 1 light Tbsp ketchup
  ⎢ 1 tsp Worcestershire sauce
  ⎢ 1 tsp chili powder
  ⎢ 1/2 tsp soy sauce
  ⎣ Pepper, to taste

4 leaves lettuce
1/4 onion
1 small tomato
1 avocado
Dash lemon juice
1/3 bunch cilantro
Shredded mozzarella cheese,
  as needed

Instructions

1. Make tortillas: in a bowl, add mixture A and whisk. Add water and stir until no clumps remain (photos 1, 2). Add oil to heated pan. Spoon batter into pan creating a 4 to 5" round tortilla (photo 3). Cook on medium heat until browned then flip (photo 4). Keep pan oiled and repeat with remaining batter.
2. Make chili filling: mince garlic. Add oil to heated pan and sauté garlic until fragrant. Add beans and sauté over high heat (photo 5). Add white wine and stir-fry. Add mixture B and stir.
3. Cut lettuce into large pieces, and dice onion. Soak in water if very pungent, then dry. Dice tomato into small cubes. Remove skin and pit from avocado (photo 6). Dice avocado and sprinkle with lemon juice. Roughly chop cilantro.
4. On separate plates, serve tortillas, chili filling, vegetables from step 3, and mozzarella cheese.

Vegetable Chop Suey

A delicious soup made from vegetables

Recipe on page 74

It doesn't have meat, but it has a rich taste that'll keep you satisfied.
Each vegetable adds a distinctive flavor to the dish. Start with the tough
vegetables and finish with the softest, so each retains its unique texture.

Shrimp and Vegetable Fritters

Crunchy from start to finish!

Recipe on page 75

The carefully picked ingredients in these fritters have a unique blend of earthy, sweet and fresh flavors. Just finish with a slow and steady fry to get a perfectly crisp outside.

Vegetable Chop Suey

Add the chives last!

Photo page 72

Ingredients (Serves 4)

1/8 head Napa cabbage
1 1/2" (3 cm) carrot, peeled
3 1/2 oz (100 g) boiled bamboo shoots
2 shiitake mushrooms
1 bunch garlic chives
1/2 bag soy (or mung) bean sprouts
1 can quail eggs (about 8 eggs)
1 Tbsp dried wood ear mushroom
1 clove garlic
1 nub ginger
A ⌈ 1 Tbsp potato (or corn) starch
　 ⌊ 2 Tbsp water
1 to 2 Tbsp sesame oil
2 Tbsp sake
1 C water
1/2 Tbsp soy sauce
Salt, pepper and sesame oil, to taste

Instructions

1. Separate stem and leaves of cabbage. Finely chop stem and cut leaves into bite-size pieces. Slice carrot into half-moons 2" (5 cm) thick. Cut bamboo shoots into 2" (5 cm) slices. Finely slice shiitake mushrooms. Cut chives into 2" (5 cm) pieces. Remove root ends from sprouts and reconstitute dried mushrooms in warm water. Mince garlic and ginger. Combine mixture A and set aside.

2. Add oil to heated pan. Sauté garlic and ginger over low heat until fragrant. Add carrots and bamboo shoots and sauté on high heat until evenly coated with oil. Add in order: sprouts, wood ear mushroom, cabbage stem, cabbage leaves and drained quail eggs.

3. When all ingredients are evenly coated with oil, add sake and stir-fry. Add water and soy sauce, then mix. Season with salt and pepper and turn off heat. Give mixture A a quick stir and then pour over contents of pan. Mix quickly and turn on heat. Cook until liquid in pan is thick.

4. Finish with sesame oil and pepper.

Shrimp and Vegetable Fritters

Cook slowly on low heat

Photo page 73

Ingredients (Serves 4)
Batter (for 1 set of fritters)

⌈ 1 C pastry flour
| 1/2 C (110 ml) water
⌊ Pinch salt

A ⌈ 1 burdock root
⌊ 1 Tbsp *aonori* dried seaweed

B | ⌈ 1 onion
| 1/2 carrot, peeled
| ⌊ 2 Tbsp *sakura* shrimp (or salad shrimp)

Salt, to taste
Oil, for frying

Instructions, part A

1. Prep vegetables: scrub burdock root, then peel into thin shavings (photo 1). Soak in lightly-vinegared water for 3 minutes.
2. In a bowl, mix flour and salt. Add water a little at a time and whisk until the batter is frothy and light (photo 2). This is batter for one set of fritters.
3. Add burdock root and seaweed, then mix until evenly coated.
4. Add appx. 1" oil to a heated pan. Add mixture from step 3 to oil and shape with a wooden spatula. Cook over medium heat until browned and crispy. Turn over and cook to desired crispiness. Remove from oil and let drain. Season with salt. Serve with tempura dipping sauce (see above).

Instructions, part B

1. Thinly slice onion and chop carrot into small pieces.
2. Follow directions above for batter and add onions, carrots and shrimp instead of burdock root and seaweed (photo 3). Follow directions in part A to finish.

Tempura Dipping Sauce Recipe

Combine 3 parts dashi, 1 part mirin and 1 part soy sauce.

1

2

3

Root Veggie Fried Rice

A fragrant delight

Recipe on 78

The vegetables in this recipe are root vegetables
that pack a serious crunch. Chop them up and
stir-fry with rice until everything's evenly mixed.
Stir-fry the whole thing until each and every grain
is nice and toasty.

Omelet Sandwich

Vietnamese-style!

Recipe on page 79

Make an omelet using dried daikon and add nam pla for that special Southeast Asian flair. The omelet and vegetables are naturally sweet. The perfect sandwich to enjoy on your day off.

Root Veggie Fried Rice

Sauté vegetables on high

Photo page 76

Ingredients (Serves 2)

6" (15 cm) burdock root
5 oz (150 g) lotus root
1 bunching onion (or green onion)
1 clove garlic
2 heaping servings steamed rice
2 Tbsp vegetable oil
Soy sauce, salt and pepper, to taste
1 Tbsp butter

Instructions

1. Peel burdock, lotus root and carrot. Dice all three into small cubes. Soak burdock and lotus root in lightly-vinegared water for about 3 minutes, then drain. Thinly slice bunching onion. Mince garlic.
2. Add oil to a heated pan. Sauté bunching onion and garlic over low heat until fragrant. Add burdock, lotus root and carrot and stir-fry on high heat.
3. When everything is evenly coated with oil, add rice. Stir-fry vegetables and rice, stirring until all ingredients are evenly mixed.
4. Season with salt, pepper and soy sauce. Remove from heat and add butter. Mix briefly then serve.

Dried Daikon Omelet Sandwich

Enjoy on a lightly-toasted baguette

Photo page 77

Ingredients (Serves 2)

1/2 oz (15 g) dried daikon
2" carrot
1/2 nub ginger
1 Tbsp sesame oil
1 Tbsp sake
1/2 tsp each nam pla (Thai fish
  sauce), sugar
A ⌈2 eggs
  ⌊Dash salt
1/2 Tbsp vegetable oil
1/2 loaf baguette bread
Butter, mayonnaise and sweet chili
  sauce, to taste
Cilantro, to taste

Instructions

1. Reconstitute dried daikon in water, then drain. Julienne carrot and ginger. Combine mixture A in a bowl and set aside. Cut root ends off cilantro.
2. Add sesame oil to a heated pan. Cook daikon, carrot and ginger on medium heat until tender. Add sake, nam pla, and sugar, then stir-fry. Place a dish over the pan and flip over, transferring vegetables to the dish.
3. Wipe pan clean and add vegetable oil. Pour mixture A into pan and stir. Let egg cook thoroughly. Add ingredients from step 2 into the middle of omelet and fold sides over, enveloping the vegetables.
4. Slice baguette in half, lightly toast, then add butter. Lay egg on bottom half of baguette and finish with chili sauce, mayonnaise and cilantro.

Tofu Steak
A succulent steak grilled on medium

Recipe on page 82

Vegetables grilled with garlic seasoning smothering a tofu steak. With melted butter, soy sauce and fresh shiso, this is an appetite-appeasing vegetarian steak. A cold tofu center is a buzz-kill, so be sure to cook thoroughly.

Lotus Root Burger
The double-punch of lotus root is great!

Recipe on page 82

Finely-chopped lotus root is crunchy, yet grated lotus root is chewy and light. When grilled into a tofu burger the veggie packs both of those textures together for a great bite. The double crunch of this lotus root burger tastes so good.

Sweet & Spicy Fried Tofu
A big serving with two distinct flavors

Recipe page 83

Tofu's deliciousness is the deliciousness of soy beans. These big chunks of golden-fried tofu are dressed with two distinctive sauces. The simply sweet dressing has a ketchup base, while the spicy one uses Doubanjiang and will give your mouth something to talk about! Let the sauces soak into the fluffy fried coating.

Tofu Steak

Fry 'til golden brown

Photo page 80

Ingredients (Serves 2)
1 block firm tofu
Flour, for dusting
1/2 bunching onion (or green onion)
1 clove garlic
2 Tbsp vegetable oil
Pinch salt
Soy sauce and pepper, to taste
1 Tbsp butter
10 leaves shiso (or basil or mint)

Instructions
1. Place tofu in a strainer and place a cutting board on top for 15 minutes to press out excess water. Remove tofu and press flour into the top and bottom. Cut bunching onions into 2" pieces. Finely chop garlic and shiso.
2. Add 1/2 Tbsp oil to heated pan. Sauté garlic over low heat until fragrant. Add bunching onion and salt, then sauté over high heat until onions are tender.
3. Heat a separate pan add 1 Tbsp of oil. Add tofu and cook, covered, over medium-low heat until browned. Flip over and continue to cook. When both sides are browned remove lid and add 1/2 Tbsp oil. Fry until crisp on both sides.
4. Serve tofu on dishes and smother with onions and garlic. Finish with butter, soy sauce, shiso and pepper.

Note
Only add flour to the top and bottom of the tofu (the surfaces that will be fried). If you cover the sides you'll end up with a pasty texture.
If using only one pan, cook tofu first and quickly fry bunching onions right after.

Lotus Root Burger

Cover and cook on low heat

Photo page 80

Ingredients (Serves 4)
1 block firm tofu
7 oz (200 g) lotus root
1/2 onion
1 tsp nutmeg
Salt and pepper, to taste
2 Tbsp vegetable oil
A ⎡ 2/3 C water
  ⎢ 2 Tbsp ketchup
  ⎢ 2 Tbsp Worcestershire sauce
  ⎢ 1 Tbsp each sake, butter
  ⎢ 1 tsp soy sauce
  ⎣ Dash pepper
Boiled potatoes and string beans, as needed

Sweet & Spicy Fried Tofu

Instructions

1. Place tofu in a strainer and place a cutting board on top for 30 minutes to squeeze out excess water.
2. Finely chop onion. Add 1 Tbsp oil to heated pan and sauté onions until transparent and lightly browned. Set aside on a dish and let cool.
3. Peel lotus root and cut in half. Take one half and chop into small pieces, then grate the other half. Soak the chopped lotus root in lightly-vinegared water for 3 minutes.
4. Add ingredients from steps 1, 2 and 3 to a bowl and mix well. Add salt, pepper and nutmeg, stirring thoroughly. Separate into 4 clumps and shape into patties. Use oil on your hands to keep patties from sticking.
5. Add 1 Tbsp oil to heated pan and lay burgers inside. Cover with a lid and cook on medium until browned. Flip over and cook until browned on other side.
6. Remove burgers from pan. In the same pan add mixture A and cook over medium-low heat, stirring frequently. Simmer until sauce thickens. Place burgers back into pan and simmer. Serve on dishes and coat with sauce. Add boiled potatoes and string beans on the side.

Note

Grate lotus root just before adding because it oxidizes quickly.

Draining the excess liquid from the tofu is necessary. The burger will fall apart if there's too much water. Wrapping tofu in paper towels will make it drain more thoroughly.

Sweet & Spicy Fried Tofu

Drain tofu well!

Photo page 81

Ingredients (Serves 4)

1 block firm tofu

A $\begin{cases} \text{1 C flour} \\ \text{2/3 C water} \end{cases}$

Flour, for dusting

Oil, for frying

1/2 head lettuce

Sweet Sauce

B $\begin{cases} \text{3 Tbsp water} \\ \text{2 Tbsp ketchup} \\ \text{2 tsp sugar} \\ \text{Pinch salt} \\ \text{Dash sesame oil} \end{cases}$

Spicy Sauce

2 shiitake mushrooms

1 bunching onion (or leek)

1/2 nub ginger

1 Tbsp sesame oil

1 to 2 Tbsp Doubanjiang (Chinese chili paste)

B $\begin{cases} \text{3 Tbsp water} \\ \text{2 Tbsp sake} \\ \text{1 Tbsp soy sauce} \\ \text{Pinch sugar} \end{cases}$

Instructions

1. Place tofu in a strainer and press with a cutting board on top for 15 minutes to squeeze out excess water (photo 1).
2. Make sweet sauce: add mixture B to a bowl and stir. Slice lettuce.
3. Next, make spicy sauce: add mixture C to a bowl and stir. Set aside. Mince shiitake mushrooms, bunching onion, and ginger. Add sesame oil to heated pan and stir in Doubanjiang. Add ginger, bunching onion, and mushroom and sauté over medium. When mushrooms are tender add mixture C, stir well, then remove from heat.
4. Add mixture A to a bowl and stir. Cut tofu into cubes and coat with mixture A. Add 1" (2 cm) oil to heated pan, then add tofu. Fry on medium heat until tofu blocks are browned on all sides (photo 2). Remove and drain excess oil. Serve tofu on two separate dishes with one sauce per dish. Serve sweet sauce tofu on a bed of lettuce.

1   **2**

Asian-style Dry Noodles

Crunchy and smooth textures at the same time

Recipe on page 86

The fried onions and peanuts pack a toothsome crunch while the lettuce and noodles give it a fresh smoothness. Mix them all together and top with sweet tomatoes, it's a smorgasbord of flavors.

Simmered Noodles with Grilled Onion

Sweet onion and curry flavor

Recipe on page 86

Sauté a heap of bunching onions in a dollop of sesame oil. Once the oil softens the onions and turns their sharp flavors into something sweeter, add curry powder and season with mirin and soy sauce. Add to bonito-infused somen noodles for a surprisingly hearty noodle dish.

Easy Cold Noodles

Best in summer!

Recipe on page 87

Broth-steeped juicy cucumbers and eggplants will quench your thirst. This is a local specialty in Miyazaki but I grew up with this dish in Osaka. It's easy to make and perfect for those "I'm too hot to eat!" days.

Asian-style Dry Noodles

Use pho noodles

Photo page 84

Ingredients (Serves 2)

3 1/2 oz (100 g) pho (rice) noodles

3 leaves lettuce

1 small tomato

1/4 bunch spring onions (or scallions)

1 Tbsp dried shrimp

2 Tbsp water

A ⌈ 1 chili pepper
  | Dash each grated garlic,
  | grated ginger
  | 1 to 2 Tbsp sesame oil
  | 1 Tbsp lemon juice
  | 1/2 Tbsp nam pla (Thai fish sauce)
  ⌊ 1 tsp sugar

Nam pla, to taste

Cilantro, peanuts and fried onions, as
needed

Instructions

1. Cook noodles according to package directions. Slice lettuce into large chunks. Dice tomato into 1" (3 cm) cubes. Cut spring onions into 2" (5 cm) pieces. Soak dried shrimp in warm water. Slice chili pepper into thin rounds (seeds included). Wrap peanuts in paper towels and crush with a rolling pin.
2. In a bowl, add mixture A and stir. Add reconstituted shrimp along with soaking water, then mix. Add noodles, lettuce, tomato and spring onions and stir. Season with nam pla.
3. Serve in dish topped with peanuts, cilantro and fried onions.

Note
Pho are Vietnamese rice noodles.
They are flat and wide, with a slick texture
and a unique taste.

Simmered Noodles with Grilled Onion

The sesame and pepper are important!

Photo page 84

Ingredients (Serves 2)

3 1/2 oz (100 g) *somen* noodles
  (or sub vermicelli)

3 C water

Handful bonito flakes

A ⌈ 1 Tbsp soy sauce
  | 1/2 Tbsp mirin (sweet cooking wine)
  ⌊ Dash each salt, sugar

3 bunching onions (or green onions)

1 Tbsp sesame oil

1 Tbsp roasted white sesame seeds

1 tsp each curry powder, soy sauce, mirin

Pepper, to taste

Instructions

1. Bring water to a boil in a pot and add bonito flakes. Reduce heat to low and simmer for 1 to 2 minutes. Use a strainer to remove flakes. Add mixture A to a bowl and stir.
2. Slice bunching onions into thin rings on the bias. Add oil to a heated pan and sauté bunching onions on high heat until tender. Add curry powder, sesame seeds, mirin, and soy sauce. Mix well and add pepper.
3. Boil *somen* noodles, rinse, then drain in a colander. Serve noodles and top with onions from step 2.

Easy Cold Noodles

Serve over barley rice

Photo page 85

Ingredients (Serves 4)

2 1/2 C water
Handful bonito flakes
2 to 3 Tbsp miso
1 eggplant (the small Japanese or Italian kind)
1 cucumber
1 *myoga* (Japanese ginger bud. Or sub ginger root)
10 shiso leaves
2 to 3 Tbsp ground white sesame seeds
1 to 2 Tbsp roasted white sesame seeds
Dash grated ginger
4 servings barley rice (white rice cooked with barley)

Instructions

1. Bring water to boil in a pot and add bonito flakes. Simmer for 1 to 2 minutes on low heat. Use a strainer to remove flakes. Add miso to water and stir to dissolve. Cover pot and refrigerate. Allow to cool completely (photo 1).
2. Cut eggplant in half lengthwise and thinly slice into half-moons. Peel a striped pattern into the cucumber and slice into thin rounds. In a bowl, mix cucumber and eggplant with salt (photo 2). Massage, then squeeze out any excess liquid, then add to chilled soup broth from step 1. Add ginger and roasted and ground sesame seeds, then return to refrigerator.
3. Julienne ginger bud and shiso.
4. When soup is completely chilled, add barley rice, then ingredients from step 2 and garnish with ginger bud and shiso.

1

2

Heartwarming Soups

Soups that will warm your body and soul with the gentle flavor of vegetables.
Hot or cold, they're quick and easy to make and very satisfying.
Just blend in the mixer and you're ready to go!

Gazpacho

**A brisk taste to wake
your taste buds!**

Recipe on page 90

Gazpacho is a mysteriously rich
soup that retains the freshness
of the vegetables that went into
it. Everything is done in the
mixer so it's very easy to make.
Have it as an appetizer and let
your stomach know you care.

Soup Trifecta

Just soup, but satisfaction guaranteed

Recipe on page 91

The colors of the veggies in these soups are very appealing. The various colors are what make these potage as fun to serve as they are to eat. *Kabocha* and soy beans, broccoli and potatoes, peppers and carrots—with these flavors and colors, you can't go wrong.

Gazpacho

Chilled to perfection!

Photo page 88

Ingredients (Serves 2)

1 tomato
1 stalk celery
1 cucumber
A ⎡ 1/2 C tomato juice
⎢ 1 to 2 Tbsp lemon juice
⎣ Dash grated garlic
Salt and pepper, to taste
Dash olive oil
2 okra

Instructions

1. Remove stem from tomato. Peel celery and cucumber. Roughly chop all vegetables.
2. Mix vegetables in a blender. When mixture is smooth, season with salt and pepper to taste.
3. Serve in dishes garnished with chopped okra and pepper.

Soup Trifecta

Don't overcook—just enough to blend the flavors

Photo page 89

Yellow Vegetable Potage

Ingredients (Serves 4)

1/4 *kabocha* (Japanese pumpkin. Or sub pumpkin)
1/2 C canned soybeans
1 C milk
A ⌈ 1 C milk
⌊ 1/2 Tbsp sugar
Salt and pepper, to taste

Instructions

1. Peel *kabocha*, remove seeds then cut into 1/2" (1 cm) cubes. Add *kabocha* and enough water to cover to a pot and simmer until tender. Add water as needed to keep from burning.
2. When tender, add *kabocha* and boiling water to a blender. Add soybeans and milk, then blend until smooth.
3. Transfer to a pan and turn on heat. Add mixture A and stir. Season with salt and pepper.

Note

You can make a chilled potage by skipping the first part of step 3 and mixing everything without heating.

Green Vegetable Potage

Ingredients (Serves 4)

1 head broccoli
1 potato
1 C milk
A ⌈ 1 C milk
⌊ 1/2 Tbsp sugar
Salt and pepper, to taste

Instructions

1. Cut broccoli into small clusters. Boil in salted water until tender, then drain. Peel potato and dice into 1/2" (1 cm) cubes. Add potato and enough water to cover to a pot and boil until tender. Add water as needed to keep from burning.
2. When tender, add potatoes and boiling water to a blender. Add broccoli and milk, then blend until smooth.
3. Transfer to a pan and turn on heat. Add mixture A and stir. Season with salt and pepper.

Note

You can make a chilled potage by skipping the first part of step 3 and mixing everything without heating.

Red Vegetable Potage

Ingredients (Serves 4)

1 carrot
1 red pepper
1 C milk
A ⌈ 1 C milk
⌊ 1/2 Tbsp sugar
Salt, pepper to taste

Instructions

1. Peel carrot and roughly chop. Remove stem and seeds of bell pepper and chop. Add vegetables and enough water to cover to a pot and boil until tender. Add water as needed to keep form burning.
2. When tender, add pumpkin and boiling water to a blender. Add milk, then blend until smooth.
3. Transfer to a pan and turn on heat. Add mixture A and stir. Season with salt and pepper.

Note

You can make a chilled potage by skipping the first part of step 3 and mixing everything without heating.

Vegetable Consommé

Rich flavors all thanks to veggies

Recipe on page 94

Slowly simmer the onion, carrot and celery. The nutrients of the vegetables will dissolve into the broth, leaving behind a satisfying, full-bodied flavor.

Watercress Soup

Bonito flakes and watercress are a fragrant mix

Recipe on page 95

The bittersweet flavor of watercress readily blends into the bonito broth. Watercress shrinks when heated, but that just means you can fit more into your bowl. This is a lovely soup that is packed with healthy goodness as well as flavor.

Scallop and Daikon Soup

A relaxing sip of sweetness

Recipe on page 95

The soymilk saturates into the daikon, giving it a wonderfully dense flavor. The sesame oil adds a soft hint of flavor that will relax you in no time.

Vegetable Consommé

Let it sit overnight for more flavor

Photo page 92

Ingredients (Serves 2 to 4)

2 stalks celery

1 carrot

1 onion

A ⌈ 1 clove garlic

Herbs, to taste (oregano, basil, rosemary,
thyme, etc.)

Salt and pepper, to taste

Instructions

1. Peel celery and carrot. Roughly chop all
   vegetables.
2. If you have an herb sachet, place mixture A
   inside.
3. Add vegetables, herbs and water to a pot and
   bring to a boil over high heat. Once boiling, turn
   to low and simmer for 1 hour. Add water as
   needed.
4. Strain soup or transfer broth to a new pot.
   Season with salt and pepper.

Note

If it boils violently the soup will turn cloudy.
Simmer it on low with very little bubbling.

Watercress Soup

Add oil just before serving

Photo page 93

Ingredients (Serves 2 to 3)

1 bunch watercress
3 C water
2 x 2" piece kelp (*konbu*)
Handful bonito flakes
1/2 nub ginger
A ⌈ 1 Tbsp mirin (sweet cooking wine)
  │ 1 tsp soy sauce
  ⌊ Salt, to taste
Vegetable oil and pepper, to taste

Instructions

1. Rinse kelp and place in a pot. Add water and turn on heat. Remove kelp just before it starts to boil. Bring to boil and add bonito flakes. Simmer for 1 to 2 minutes then strain. Add mixture A.
2. Mince ginger. Cut root ends off watercress. Add each to pot and simmer briefly. Serve and garnish with oil and pepper.

Scallop and Daikon Soup

The blend of ginger and sesame oil is key

Photo page 93

Ingredients (Serves 2 to 3)

2 1/2" daikon (with leaves, if possible)
2 1/2 oz (70 g) scallops, canned
1 nub ginger
1 Tbsp sesame oil
2 Tbsp sake
2 C milk
Salt and pepper, to taste
Sesame oil, to taste

Instructions

1. Peel daikon and slice into 1 1/4" (3 cm) rounds. Cut rounds into four equal pieces. Mince ginger.
2. Add oil to heated pan and sauté ginger over low heat until fragrant. Add daikon and sauté on high heat until evenly coated with oil. Add scallops (including canning liquid) and stir, then add sake and stir-fry.
3. Add milk. When milk boils turn heat to low and simmer until daikon is tender. Add salt and pepper and serve garnished with shredded daikon leaves. Drizzle with sesame oil, if desired.

Parsley and *Aburaage* Soup

The adult-friendly flavor of parsley

Recipe page 98

One day, after becoming an adult, I realized how good parsley is. As a child I never really gave a thought to it. Here I show off parsley in a simple salt-based soup.

Silken Tofu Soup

Smooth tofu, dense soup

Recipe page 98

A thick, bonito-based soup with chunks of smooth tofu—this is a soup that goes down easy and warms you up. The gelatinous soup matches well with the silky tofu.

Korean-style Stew

Refreshingly spicy

Recipe page 98

The richness of vegetables with a bunch of spice. As an excellent side dish to balance a heavy, meaty meal of *yakiniku*, your stomach will thank you.

Komatsuna Soup

The aroma of sesame with sweet veggie flavors

Recipe page 99

Simply frying up vegetables before simmering will create a great soup. The secret to an even better soup is adding fried mochi. It's truly the perfect combination. Try it and see for yourself.

Parsley and *Aburaage* Soup

Get the deep-fried tofu crispy in a toaster oven

Photo page 96

Ingredients (Serves 2 to 3)

1 sheet *aburaage* (thin fried tofu)
1 stalk parsley
3 C water
Handful bonito flakes
A ⌈ 1 to 2 Tbsp oil
⌊ Salt and pepper, to taste

Instructions

1. Slice *aburaage* into 2" (5 cm) pieces and crisp in a toaster oven. Remove bottom 1" (3 cm) from parsley stalks, then cut the rest into 2 to 3 pieces.
2. Bring water to a boil. Add bonito flakes and simmer for 1 to 2 minutes on low heat. Use a strainer to remove bonito flakes, squeezing liquid back into pot. Add mixture A, then add parsley and simmer. Pour into dishes, add tofu, and sprinkle with pepper.

Silken Tofu Soup

Turn off the heat while you add the starch

Photo page 96

Ingredients (Serves 2 to 3)

1/2 block silken tofu
1/4 stalk *mitsuba* (or watercress or chervil)
A ⌈ 1 Tbsp potato (or corn) starch
⌊ 2 Tbsp water
3 C water
Handful bonito flakes
B ⌈ 1/2 Tbsp each soy sauce, mirin
⌈ (sweet cooking wine)
⌊ Salt, to taste
Dash each sesame oil, grated ginger
Roasted white sesame seeds, as desired

Instructions

1. Cut *mitsuba* into 1" (3 cm) pieces. Combine mixture A.
2. Bring water to a boil, add bonito flakes, and simmer for 1 to 2 minutes on low heat. Use a strainer to remove bonito flakes, squeezing out liquid back into the pot. Add mixture B and simmer.
3. Cut tofu into bite-size pieces and add to soup broth. Turn off heat, stir mixture A briefly then add to soup and stir immediately. When soup thickens, add *mitsuba* and stir. Serve in bowls and finish with sesame oil, ginger and roasted sesame seeds.

Korean-style Stew

Split the kimchi into 2 batches!

Photo page 97

Ingredients (Serves 2 to 3)

1/8 stock Napa cabbage
1/2 bunch edible chrysanthemum (aka chop suey greens. Or sub. spinach)
1 bunching onion (or green onion)
2 cloves garlic
1 piece *aburaage* (thin fried tofu)
7 oz (200 g) Napa cabbage kimchi
1 Tbsp sesame oil
1/2 Tbsp gochujang (Korean pepper paste)
3 chili peppers
1 Tbsp sake
3 C water
1 Tbsp miso
Soy sauce and roasted white sesame seeds, to taste

Komatsuna Soup

Add the *komatsuna* last

Photo page 97

Instructions

1. Separate cabbage stem and leaves. Thinly slice stem and cut leaves into bite-size pieces. Cut chrysanthemum into 2" (5 cm) pieces. Cut bunching onion into rounds 2/5" (1 cm) wide. Mince garlic. Cut *aburaage* into 2/5" (1 cm) strips. Cut kimchi into bite-size pieces if too large. Remove stems from chili peppers and shred.
2. Add oil to heated pan and sauté garlic until fragrant. Add gochujang and chili peppers then stir. Add bunching onion and sauté over high heat.
3. When bunching onions are lightly charred, add sake and stir-fry. Add water and cook over medium-low heat. Add *aburaage*, cabbage stems, half of the kimchi, cabbage leaves and miso, in that order. Simmer for 2 to 3 minutes.
4. Add soy sauce gradually, checking flavor repeatedly. Add chrysanthemum, remaining half of kimchi and sesame seeds, and stir.

Note

In warmer months, try using spring or summer vegetables like garlic chives or parsley. The first batch of kimchi gives the broth flavor while the second half gives it a great crunch.

Ingredients (Serves 4)

1/3 bunch *komatsuna* (or mustard greens, spinach or bok choy)
1/2" burdock root
1 bunching onion
3 1/2 oz (100 g) taro root (or sub. parsnip)
1 Tbsp sesame oil
3 C water
Handful bonito flakes
1/2 to 1 Tbsp mirin (sweet cooking wine)
Soy sauce, to taste
4 blocks mochi (pounded rice cakes)
Seven-spice powder, to taste
Oil, for frying

Instructions

1. Add water to a pot and bring to a gentle boil. Add bonito flakes and simmer on low for 1 to 2 minutes. Use a strainer to remove bonito flakes, squeezing liquid back into the pot.
2. Remove root ends from *komatsuna* and cut into 2" (5 cm) pieces. Shave burdock root into thin slices with a peeler and soak in lightly vinegared water for at least 3 minutes, then pat dry. Peel carrots and slice into thin half-moons. Slice bunching onion into 1/3" wide rounds.
3. Add sesame oil to a heated pan. Add bunching onion, burdock root, carrot and taro, in that order. Stir-fry over high heat.
4. When all ingredients are coated with oil, turn off heat and add to pot with soup broth. Simmer over low heat for 5 to 6 minutes.
5. Add *komatsuna* and mix, then add mirin. Add soy sauce gradually, checking flavor repeatedly.
6. Cut mochi into halves. Add 3/4" (2 cm) of oil to a heated pan, wait until oil is heated then add mochi. Fry until browned on both sides. Add to soup and garnish with seven-spice powder.

Pasta! Pasta!

Pasta and vegetables go great together. When onions and a box of pasta are all that's left in the cupboard you can still make a great meal. Fresh vegetables and cooked pasta are a specialty.

Fettuccine with Onions and Olives

Soak in the oniony sweetness

Recipe page 102

It's the onions that make this so good. Fill a pan with onions, sauté 'em and watch them shrink down. The sweetness and bitterness of the onion achieves a perfect balance for a taste you can't beat. Onions are just that good.

Penne with Broccoli and Basil

Boiled broccoli as pasta dressing

Recipe on page 102

Take the whole broccoli from stem to floret and chop finely. Simmer until the broccoli dissolves into the broth. An easy recipe for a refreshing broccoli-based dish!

Capellini and Fresh Tomatoes

Tomatoes give a sweet coolness

Recipe page 103

Cook the pasta a little longer than listed on the package so when it's refrigerated the pasta doesn't clump up. If you can't get your hands on plum tomatoes use cherry or regular beef-steak. Either way, it's delicious.

Fettuccine with Onions and Olives

Onions turn bitter when charred, so be careful!

Photo page 100

Ingredients (Serves 2)
6 1/2 oz (180 g) fettuccine
2 onions
10 black olives, pitted
2 cloves garlic
2 to 3 Tbsp olive oil
Salt and pepper, to taste

Instructions
1. Halve onions lengthwise, then slice thinly. Mince garlic after removing any green cores. Slice olives into rings.
2. Add olive oil to heated pan. Sauté onion and garlic on high heat until onions are tender and fragrant. Add olives and stir. Add salt and pepper to taste.
3. Cook fettuccine according to package directions. Drain in a colander and add to pan with vegetables. Stir and serve on dishes. Sprinkle with pepper.

Note
Fettuccine is thinner than spaghetti, so the cooking time is shorter, making it very convenient.

Penne with Broccoli and Basil

Add the basil after you turn off the heat

Photo page 101

Ingredients (Serves 2)
4 oz (120 g) penne
1 head broccoli
10 leaves basil
1 clove garlic
2 Tbsp each olive oil, white wine
Parmesan cheese, as needed
Salt, pepper and olive oil, to taste

Instructions

1. Start cooking penne according to package directions.
2. Cut 1" (2 cm) root end of broccoli and peel stem. Finely chop broccoli. Shred basil leaves and mince garlic. If using a block of Parmesan, grate desired amount.
3. Add olive oil to a heated pan. Add garlic and sauté over low heat until fragrant. Add broccoli, season with salt and pepper and sauté over high heat. Add white wine and stir-fry. Add 4 to 5 ladlefuls of pasta boiling water and simmer broccoli until tender. Season with salt and pepper while checking flavor.
4. Remove pasta from water and drain, then add to pan with vegetables. Stir pasta into sauce. Turn off heat and add basil and stir briefly. Serve pasta and finish with olives, parmesan cheese, salt and pepper.

Note

Penne are small tube-shaped pasta, and the boiling time is on the long side.

Capellini and Fresh Tomatoes

Thinly slice tomatoes!

Photo page 101

Ingredients (Serves 2)

6 1/2 oz (180 g) capellini
3 cherry or plum tomatoes
10 shiso leaves (or basil or mint)
A ⌈ Dash grated garlic
  | 1 to 2 Tbsp olive oil
  ⌊ 1 Tbsp lemon juice
Salt, pepper and olive oil, to taste

Instructions

1. Thinly slice tomatoes and shred shiso leaves. Add mixture A to a bowl and stir, then set aside.
2. Cook capellini a little longer than indicated by package directions. Drain, add to ice water to set, then drain again when cooled.
3. Add tomato, shiso leaves and pasta to bowl with mixture A. Stir well. Season with salt and pepper as needed. Serve on dishes and finish with olive oil.

Note

Capellini is often called "angel hair" since it's a very thin pasta. It's often used in cold pasta dishes.

Cabbage and Anchovy Pasta
Boil the cabbage with the pasta

Recipe page 107

Right before the pasta is done cooking, add the cabbage and give it a quick boil. The tender sweetness of the cabbage is subtle while the anchovies give it a kick. It's easy to make and very scrumptious.

Carbonara with Spring Onions
Blue cheese dressing gives this dish a unique flavor

Recipe page 106

Take the fresh and fragrant spring onion, and mix it with sautéed garlic and blue cheese for a rich and powerful sauce. A delectable treat, and a unique carbonara.

104

Creamy Veggie Pasta

A smooth, creamy sauce

Recipe page 107

To make this pasta, just blend roasted pine nuts and boiled asparagus and voilà!—a smooth texture and fresh-yet-rich sauce that will leave your mouth happy.

Carbonara with Spring Onions

Turn off the heat, add egg and stir quickly

Photo page 104

Ingredients (Serves 2)

6 1/2 oz (180 g) spaghetti
1/2 bunch spring onions (or scallions)
1 clove garlic
1/2 oz (15 g) Gorgonzola cheese
A ⌈ 1 egg
⌊ 5 Tbsp Parmesan cheese
1 Tbsp olive oil
1 Tbsp white wine
4/5 C fresh cream
Salt, pepper and Parmesan cheese,
 to taste

Instructions

1. Cut spring onions into 2" (5 cm) pieces. Finely chop garlic. Dice Gorgonzola cheese into 1/2" cubes. Combine mixture A and set aside.

2. Add olive oil to heated pan and sauté garlic over low heat until browned. Add spring onions and cook over medium heat. When oil has evenly coated the onions, add wine and stir briefly. Promptly add cream and Gorgonzola cheese. Simmer over lower heat until smooth.

3. Follow instructions on spaghetti package and cook pasta. Drain pasta, then add to pan with vegetables. Mix then season with salt and pepper. Turn off heat and mix well. Plate and serve with pepper and Parmesan cheese.

Cabbage and Anchovy Spaghetti

Boil the cabbage for 20 seconds

Photo page 104

Ingredients (Serves 2)

6 1/2 oz (180 g) spaghetti
1/4 head (small) cabbage
2 anchovies
A ⌈ Dash grated garlic
   ⌊ 1 to 2 Tbsp olive oil
Salt and pepper, to taste

Instructions

1. Julienne cabbage into strips and chop anchovies.
2. Combine mixture A in a bowl. Add anchovies and stir.
3. Cook spaghetti according to package directions. Add cabbage 20 seconds before pasta is done, then drain both in a colander. Add to bowl with mixture A and stir. Season to taste with salt and pepper.

Pasta in Asparagus Cream Sauce

Roast pine nuts for a pleasurable fragrance

Photo page 105

Ingredients (Serves 2)

6 1/2 oz (180g) tagliatelle (or fettuccine)
1 bunch asparagus
  ⌈ Dash grated garlic
  │ 1 Tbps olive oil
A │ 1/4 C milk
  │ 2 Tbsp pine nuts
  ⌊ 1/3 tsp salt
1/2 C fresh cream
Salt and pepper, to taste

Instructions

1. Cut asparagus in half and boil in salted water for 30 seconds then drain. Add pine nuts to a heated pan and dry roast.
2. In a blender, add all ingredients from mixture A and step 1, then blend. Transfer to a pan, turn on heat, add cream and stir.
3. Follow directions on pasta package and cook pasta. Drain and add to 2, season with salt and pepper.

Note

Tagliatelle is a flat and thin pasta like fettuccine. It goes well with thick sauces.

Reference Guide

Common Ingredients in Japanese Cooking

Mirin (sweet, seasoned rice wine)
Can be found in finer grocery stores and Asian markets.
Substitutions
1 tbsp dry sherry + 1/2 tsp sugar.
Or, use sweet sherry.
Or, heat two parts sake and one part sugar.

Fried Tofu (*aburaage* and *atsuage*)
Aburaage is a thin sheet of fried tofu. It can be stuffed with rice to make Inari sushi.
Atsuage is a block of thick, fried tofu. House Foods makes a product called Tofu Cutlet which can be substituted for either.

Miso (soybean paste)
Can be found in finer grocery stores and Asian markets.

Seven-Spice Powder (*shichimi togarashi*, *nanami togarashi*)
Can be found in Asian markets.
Substitution: Cayenne pepper

Sake (rice wine)
Substitutions: white wine, white cooking wine

Mitsuba (trefoil, honewort)
Substitutions: watercress, chervil

Shiso (perilla, beefsteak plant)
Substitutions: basil, mint

Recipes for Common Components

Tsukudani **Broth**
Most commonly used to prepare *konbu* seaweed.
Ingredients:
3 Tbsp soy sauce
3 Tbsp sake
2 Tbsp sugar
2 Tbsp mirin
Add everything to a pot, bring to a boil to dissolve sugar. Add *konbu* (or other ingredient) and reduce heat to low and simmer.

Noodle sauce (*men tsuyu*)
1/2 C (100 ml) water
1 Tbsp soy sauce
1 Tbsp each sugar and mirin

Roasted Sesame Seeds
Place sesame seeds in a single layer on a sheet pan and roast in a 350° oven for about 10 minutes. Cool and store in an airtight container.

Online Resources

To buy ingredients

www.asianfoodgrocer.com
www.koamart.com
www.savoryspiceshop.com
www.japansuper.com
www.sushifoods.com

For information on ingredients and substitutions

www.foodsubs.com
(aka The Cook's Thesaurus)
www.gourmetsleuth.com
www.asiafood.org

Kentaro Kobayashi

Born 1972 in Tokyo, Japan. Kentaro began working as an illustrator while attending Musashino College of Fine Arts, and simultaneously put his inborn love of cooking to work by becoming a culinary artist. In addition to charismatically introducing recipes on television and in magazines, he helped develop ready-made recipes for retail sale and also hosted cooking classes, among other various activities. Kentaro's motto is "Easy and delicious, stylish yet realistic." In particular he proposes menus and meal plans based on what he himself wants to eat and make, in keeping with his lifestyle and the idea of always being practical. This book is written from that perspective and draws on the author's own personal experience.

Veggie Haven

Translation: Jessica Bezer
Vetting: Glory Gallo

Published by Vertical, Inc., New York.

Originally published in Japanese as *Yasai Bakkari* by Bunka Shuppankyoku, Tokyo, 2003.

ISBN 978-1-934287-62-0

Manufactured in The United States of America

First American Edition

Vertical, Inc.
www.vertical-inc.com

Donburi Mania

978-1-934287-49-1
$14.95/$16.95

Noodle Comfort

978-1-934287-57-6
$14.95/$17.50

Bento Love

978-1-934287-58-3
$14.95/$17.50

Veggie Haven

978-1-934287-62-0
$14.95/$17.50

O お MA 任 KA せ SE!!

★ IRON CHEF CHEN'S ★
KNOCKOUT CHINESE
★ CHEN KENICHI ★

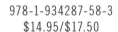

Iron Chef Chen's Knockout Chinese
978-1-934287-46-0, $19.95/$22.95
Cook like an Iron Chef! Dozens of unbeatable recipes from the undisputed champion of the original Kitchen Stadium, Iron Chef Chinese Chen Kenichi.

978-1-934287-63-7
$14.95/$17.50

The *Easy Japanese Cooking* Series
Contemporary Japanese dishes made simple!
Kentaro's quick and easy recipes bring flavorful, filling meals to your home.

Leave your culinary needs to Vertical's seven-course menu of Japanese cookbooks. Save your airfare; we've brought over the best Japan's kitchens have to offer.

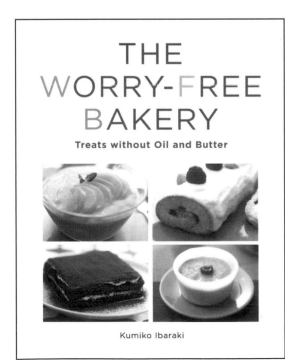

THE
WORRY-FREE
BAKERY
Treats without Oil and Butter

Kumiko Ibaraki

The Worry-Free Bakery: Treats Without Oil and Butter
978-1-934287-69-9, $14.95/$18.95
Tasty cakes and cookies without the guilt and fat! 45 lip-smacking low-calorie snacks that warm the heart while being light-on-the-hips.

V
E
R
T
I
C
A
L.